D1595352

"*Shoot from the Heart* is the book I wish I [...]
Diane is a wealth of knowledge and exp[...]
filmmaker, from film student to seasoned pro.

—Alex Ferrari, Writer/Director and Founder of IndieFilmHustle.com

"Diane Bell is the voice of our generation. As a filmmaker she has
blazed a trail and I know firmly that her words in this book will help
heal the world."

—Marianna Palka, actor (in *Glow*), writer/director: *Good Dick; Bitch*

"Diane Bell, a filmmaker who has always operated from a place of
authenticity, instinct and grace has written a bible that crystallizes the
basic truths of making your independent film."

—Valerie Weiss, independent feature filmmaker (*A Light Beneath Their Feet; The
Archer*) and television director (*Suits; Chicago MD; Scandal*)

"If you are a filmmaker who wants to spend more time making films
than asking for permission, this is the book for you."

—Emily Best, founder/CEO of Seed & Spark

"This guide was a roadmap to me getting off the couch and launching
my dreams and career into reality. Diane taught me you don't have to
sell your soul to Hollywood to make a great film with heart."

—Alicia J. Rose, director (*The Benefits of Gusbandry*)

"In the ever-changing landscape of indie filmmaking, *Shoot from the
Heart* offers a detailed blueprint for making your best work and getting it out there. A must-read for anyone hoping to have a sustainable
career as an independent filmmaker today."

—Jon Reiss, filmmaker (*Bomb It*), self-distribution consultant, and author of *Think
Outside the Box Office*

"A bulletproof step-by-step on how to turn what's in your heart into a
movie and then share it with the world."

—Bryan Larkin, BAFTA Scotland award-winning director (*Reflections of a Life,
Running in Traffic* and *Scene*)

"A book that is like film school in your pocket."

—Laurie Collyer, director (*Sherrybaby; Sunlight Jr., Furlough*)

"It confirmed everything I knew about indie filmmaking, and it empowered me with more confidence and tools for my next project. This book is essential reading for any filmmaker."
—Jessie McCormack, screenwriter and director (*Expecting, Piss Off I Love You*)

"The well laid-out plan in this guide will not only assist filmmakers on their journey, but will motivate them to get started and give them the courage they need to keep on when it gets tough. If I can do it, so can you."
—Barri Chase, screenwriter and director (*The Watchman's Canoe, Coyote Howls*)

"If you are truly ready to make a film, this is the book for you. It's a very practical, step-by-step how-to book with realistic advice and savvy insight to the fast changing indie-prod world. ."
—Paul Chitlik, writer/producer/director (*The Wedding Dress; The New Twilight Zone; Alien Abduction*), author of *Rewrite: A Step-by-Step Guide to Strengthen Structure, Characters, and Drama in Your Screenplay*

"If the goal is to have a finished, completed product that you personalize with your best intent, talent, and focus, *Shoot From the Heart* will be part of your crew."
—Iram Parveen Bilal, international director/writer/producer (*Josh; Forbidden Steps*)

"A firm foundation for anyone looking to realize their first independent feature film."
—Raindance Film Festival

"An invaluable resource for filmmakers about to make their first low -budget feature."
—Kim Adelman, instructor low-budget filmmaking, UCLA Extension and author of *Making It Big in Shorts*

"Diane Bell has written a book that will inspire you, instruct you and inform you. You'll learn how to get the right people on board your project for each job. Let's face it, anyone can make a movie, but with Bell's advice you can make an amazing movie. Her lessons on filmmaking are enlightening, frank, and well thought out."
—Forris Day Jr. host of *Rolling Tape* filmmakers interview show and guest analyst on the *Hitch 20* podcast

SHOOT FROM THE HEART

SUCCESSFUL FILMMAKING FROM A SUNDANCE REBEL

DIANE BELL

MICHAEL WIESE PRODUCTIONS

Published by Michael Wiese Productions
12400 Ventura Blvd. #1111
Studio City, CA 91604
(818) 379-8799, (818) 986-3408 (Fax)
mw@mwp.com
www.mwp.com
Manufactured in the
United States of America

This book was set in Arno Pro, Eveleth, and Whitney

Cover design: Johnny Ink. johnnyink.com
Interior design: Debbie Berne
Copyediting: Sherry Parnes
Cover photograph: Mati Young
Cover model: Kristine Dunnigan

ISBN: 978-1-615932-887

Library of Congress Cataloging-in-Publication Data
Names: Bell, Diane.
Title: Shoot from the heart: a rebel's guide to filmmaking from funding to
    distribution / by Diane Bell.
Description: Studio City, CA: Michael Wiese Productions, [2018]
Identifiers: LCCN 2018013960 | ISBN 9781615932887
Subjects: LCSH: Motion pictures—Production and direction.
Classification: LCC PN1995.9.P7 B3535 2018 | DDC 791.4302/32--dc23
LC record available at https://lccn.loc.gov/2018013960

CONTENTS

THANKS

They say it takes a village to make a movie, and as anyone who's sat through the end credits of one can testify, it sometimes takes a whole damn city. Surprise! It's the same for a book, even though only one name shows up on the cover.

First, this wouldn't exist without Ken Lee and Michael Wiese who took a leap of faith with me. They are the most awesome publishers a writer could hope for and have created a company that has published so many of the books that have inspired me and guided me as a filmmaker. I'm honored to be in their company.

Second, huge thanks to my manager Dan Halsted who has stood by me even as I make the craziest choices in my life and career. To have someone who appreciates that following your heart is the most important thing you can do is everything.

Next, I need to thank everyone who has attended one of the Rebel Heart Film Workshops, which allowed to me to develop this program. You rebels inspire me so much and make me feel so passionately about what I do. Seeing you succeed gives my greatest joy. Love you all. Make more movies and let's change the world, one film at a time.

This book wouldn't be what it is without the input of some early readers. Sibyl Gardner and Neil Krolicki, I cannot thank you enough.

Also thanks to Jon Reiss for your generous support and encouragement. You are a hero of the new model of filmmaking.

Then there are the people who make it all possible, and not only that, but who make it all worthwhile; the ones who make you smile everyday and give your life meaning. Huge gratitude to my parents, Anne and Richard Bell always, and to my sisters, Caroline and Susan.

To my sons, Tennyson and Theo, the most glorious distractions from writing and filmmaking in the world: I love you both with all my heart.

And finally to my husband: Chris Byrne, you are my sun, my moon, my everything. I dedicate this book to you, because without you, I never would have had the courage to make a film. Every filmmaker needs a huge believer in their lives; you are mine. Thank you.

FOREWORD

LEAH MEYERHOFF
founder of Film Fatales

Cinema is a tool for empathy, allowing us to relate to perspectives different from our own. Audiences are hungry for bold new voices. To tell the stories of the world, we need filmmakers who reflect its composition.

Since the birth of the movie industry, powerful gatekeepers have chosen not only which stories get to be told, but also who gets to tell them. But these systems are shifting. Now anyone with a camera can make a movie, but the flood of content makes it harder than ever to make one that stands out.

As the founder of Film Fatales, a global network of women feature film and television directors, I have seen first-hand the many obstacles that independent filmmakers face—particularly those from underrepresented communities—in getting their films made and seen.

Enter *Shoot From the Heart*, a manifesto that leads filmmakers through the journey of making a movie and empowers them to make the best one possible. This book is inspiring, truthful and packed full of the knowledge you need to make it happen. Together, we can change the narrative.

INTRODUCTION

If you are ready to stop talking about making a movie and actually *make* your damn movie, you have picked up the right book. And let's be clear: I hope you're ready not just to make any old movie, but to make a kick-ass, standout, knock 'em down, award-winning movie that you will be proud of for the rest of your life.

Why not?

If you're going to work your butt off for a year or two making it (and that's what it's going to take), you might as well aim super high, empower yourself with the knowledge you need and *make it happen*. No more excuses.

Essentially, this book is the end of all your lame excuses. Don't know what to make your movie about? We'll deal with that. No contacts in the industry? Got that covered. Or the big one: Don't know how to get the money? You will never be able to complain about that again. Trust me.

Here's the thing: Millions of people dream about making a movie, literally millions, but then they get scared. It's far easier to be a brilliant filmmaker in your mind, rather than actually take the risk of making something. I know what it's like: you don't know where to start. It seems overwhelming. The doubts creep in: Where can you get the money? You live in a small town, and you've never even met a filmmaker! Who the hell are you to make a movie?!

Who the hell are you *not* to—if it's your dream?

You can do it. I know you can, because I've done it, and I'm not special in any way (except perhaps to my family!). I don't have a trust fund, and I was born in Dumfries, Scotland, which is about as far from Hollywood as Mars. But I did it. Without connections in the industry or wealthy relatives, I made a film that was selected for Sundance, won awards, opened doors, and took my career to a different level. I also had the time of my life making it. Since then, I've made two more films, and I intend to make many more. There is a way to do this that not only gets your movie made, but sets up the situation where you can do it again and again, for the rest of your life, regardless of whether or not you knock it out of the park the first time. For real.

In this book, you are going to learn a way to develop, finance, produce and distribute films that is completely self-starting and can be done by anyone, anywhere. If you are willing to do the work, you can have your dream career as a filmmaker.

Until very recently, to have such a career meant you had to move to LA or New York, and once you were there, you had to be chosen by the gatekeepers of the industry. If they didn't select you, you had no hope, and if you didn't look like them (i.e., white cisgender male—and yo! If that's you, there ain't nothing wrong with it! Just as there ain't nothing wrong with being female, LBGTQ, POC etc.; plenty of space at this party for everyone), forget about it. The great thing about being alive right now is that this is no longer the case. If you want a career making movies, there is absolutely nothing to stop you except your own fear and a lack of the nuts-and-bolts knowledge you need. The crazy thing, however, is many aspiring filmmakers still have their heads stuck in the old conventional way of doing things. The result? They never make a feature film at all, or they make one that doesn't quite work out, and then give up and go back to the day job.

Let's talk briefly about what the conventional path is in today's world, and how it usually plays out. You write a script, take it to production companies, and try to sell it. You pitch it at contests and festivals. You write query letters, meet with agents, and you try to attach named talent, so that you have a package for raising finance. You find out that your best friend went to school with an A-list actor, and he says he can get it to them. You're thrilled, but then wait months for a response. Another friend knows someone who's on a TV show, and so you send the script to them, even though they're not quite right for your project. Still, you hope they'll respond to it and wait months for a response.

Time keeps passing—months, years slipping by, and while no one firmly commits to make your movie, everyone encourages you, even as they suggest changes you should make to it; and you keep doing that—making those changes, even when your heart isn't in them. You are convinced that once you get these people to sign on, these powerful people, your movie will be made, you'll make a million bucks, and you'll be rehearsing your Oscar speech for real.

It could happen that way. Anything is possible, and I'm not here to tell you it isn't. In fact, quite the opposite: I'm convinced that nothing is impossible in this business. It's almost my mantra. But it's also true that you could be waiting for the next ten years to get your movie off the ground; waiting so long that you forget why you ever even wanted to make it in the first place. You have no control over how long it will take, because you have given your power away. You are waiting for the powers that be to greenlight you, instead of greenlighting yourself.

The most incredible, mind-blowing thing about the world today for filmmakers is that, for the first time in history, not only is it possible to make an awesome film for a relatively small amount of money (a movie that no one is going to watch and think: *Wow, I've had dinners that cost more than that*), but it is also possible for you to sell it. The distribution of films has always been next to impossible without the backing of a major company; but now, with the advent of online streaming, you can sell your film directly to the audience and make serious money.

What you're going to learn in this book is a new, self-empowered model for making and distributing your movie. You raise the money you need, and you make the movie you want to make. No compromises. You have an awesome, inspired, creatively fulfilling time doing it. You plan the distribution from day one, so that you make money from your film, and here's the best part: You get to do it again, as often as you like, for the rest of your life.

The aim is not to make a single film, but to make many. To create the situation in which you can keep making them, no matter what. There's often huge pressure on filmmakers to hit a home run with their very first movie, which is totally nuts and utterly unhelpful. Like any art or craft, filmmaking needs to be practiced in order to be mastered. Hitchcock made over thirty films before he made *Rear Window*. Ingmar Bergman had made eighteen films before *The Seventh Seal*. More recently, Sean Baker has been lauded for *The Florida Project*, his seventh film. The idea that we make a masterpiece on our first outing is ludicrous. Sure, some people pull it off (Orson Welles is the patron saint of that club, debuting with *Citizen Kane*, which is still considered one of the best movies ever)—but they are the exception, not the rule.

Many filmmakers manage to make one movie, and when it doesn't set the world on fire, they give up. They've often maxed out their credit cards, or remortgaged their house to make that movie, and they can't imagine how they could ever make another one anyway, they're so deep in debt. To me, this is a crying shame, because how many of those filmmakers might have become a Hitchcock or a Bergman, if only they had had the chance to continue? What I'm proposing is a method in which you don't use your own money, and that you plan so that no matter how your first film turns out (or your second or your third), you'll get the chance to learn your lessons from it and do it again. So that you can keep getting better at what you do, until one day one of your films legit does start a box office, award-winning inferno.

The method I'm going to share here is largely based on my own experiences, both good and bad, making my first feature, *Obselidia* (And if you're reaching for your dictionary, thinking, *what the heck is that weird word*, stop right there. I made it up, and for the record, it's an encyclopedia of obsolete things). This film was made for $140,000 using private equity finance

The poster for my first
feature film, *Obselidia*

that I raised myself, with no star names or connections. It was made as far off the conventional film-world grid as you can imagine, and yet *Obselidia* premiered in competition at the Sundance Film Festival, where it won two awards. It went on to play successfully at film festivals around the world, and was nominated for two Independent Spirit Awards.

In this book, I will share with you exactly how I've done it, step by simple step, giving you a manageable blueprint of how to make it happen yourself. It's a rebellious model, because it doesn't fly with conventional wisdom of how to go about making a movie. But it works, and there's nothing to stop you except your own doubt. From dreaming about making a movie to watching that movie premiere at Sundance took

Winning an award at Sundance—nope, I wasn't emotional; you're imagining it.

little more than a year for me, and seriously: It could be the same for you.

Obviously, I can't guarantee that your film will get into Sundance, sell for a million and win big awards. No one can guarantee that, and I know that I was super lucky. But what I can guarantee is that if you follow the steps in this book, you will make your film—or, at the very least, you will lose all your excuses for not doing it. And if you really pay attention, you won't just make one film, but you will hold the keys to a successful career as a filmmaker, should you wish for that.

Let's talk briefly about what real success looks like. There are many lies in the film industry, and they do filmmakers no service. These lies make it seem like there is one single path to filmmaking success (*you need $5 million and recognizable name talent*), and if you don't follow that path, you might as well give up. They make it seem like the only successful career in filmmaking is the one where you move from the $100,000 movie to the million-dollar movie to the ten million-dollar movie to directing *Batman,* which obviously worked great for Chris Nolan, but won't work for most of us. However, that doesn't mean we should give up and go home.

There is another way, a different model. I'm going to share with you the naked truth about indie filmmaking, as someone who has made three feature films in eight years. I will endeavor to peel back the myths that make success in indie filmmaking so incredibly elusive, the lies that keep filmmakers afraid, and chasing a dream they can never catch.

I'm never going to say that the path I'm sharing is the only way to succeed, or that you shouldn't try other methods. At the core of what I've learned is this: Only you know your movie, and the path it needs to be birthed into the world. And the number one thing you have to do, if you're going to succeed with your movie, is to trust your instincts. In your heart, you already know what you need to do. If you know that you need $10 million dollars to make your movie, go for it. Be smart and strategic, and don't rest until you get it.

I truly believe making films is like making babies. As the parent of a child, you know them better than anyone in the world, and it's your job to nurture them and help them grow as best you can. So too with making films. Just as there are many ways to raise a happy baby, and what works for one kid will be different for another, there's no single prescription to making movies that works for everyone, all the time. But the path I'm proposing has been tried and tested. It's worked for me, and for many people with whom I have shared it with at workshops.

There's absolutely no reason it can't work for you too. If you are truly ready to take your destiny in your own hands, follow these sixteen steps and make your damn movie now.

ABOUT THIS BOOK

The book is organized, by chapter, into the sixteen steps that I think are essential for making and distributing a standout indie film. It provides an easy-to-reference plan to keep you on track as you start the process of making a film.

I recommend reading the whole book beforehand, so that you can get an overview of the journey on which you are heading. Then go back and use it as a reference and inspiration while you actually go on your filmmaking journey.

You may already have a script you love and want to make, and if so, you can skip the part about screenwriting. If you've already raised finance, you can skip everything up to that point. It's totally fine to start wherever you are in the process, but understand that if you read this from start to finish, there will be a powerful effect, so I encourage you to read parts from the beginning, even if you feel like you're past them.

At the end of each chapter is a bullet point list of actions to take. These are the *microsteps* within each step, and they should help you stay on track and get your film made.

Throughout the book you'll also learn the conventional path vs. the path with a rebel heart. As stated before, I would never tell you the latter is always the best for you, but if you are ready to make a movie on your own terms, and don't want to wait another minute, trust me: the rebel heart path is always the way to go.

THE SIXTEEN STEPS

☐ *Step 1.* Develop a Singular Script

☐ *Step 2.* Set a Start Date

☐ *Step 3.* Find a Line Producer

☐ *Step 4.* Lock Down a Schedule and Budget

☐ *Step 5.* Write a Business Plan

☐ *Step 6.* Find a DP, Editor and Key Cast

☐ *Step 7.* Shoot an Awesome Teaser Trailer

☐ *Step 8.* Start an LLC/ Raise the Money

☐ *Step 9.* Crowdfund: You Must Do It!

☐ *Step 10.* Recruit Your Crew

☐ *Step 11.* Cast Your Smaller Roles

☐ *Step 12.* Pre-production Essentials: You Can't Plan Too Much!

☐ *Step 13.* Get your Movie "In the Can"

☐ *Step 14.* Post-production Essentials: Editing, Music, Sound, Color

☐ *Step 15.* Submit to Festivals

☐ *Step 16.* Execute your Distribution Plan

STEP 1
DEVELOP A
SINGULAR
SCRIPT

"To make a great film you
 need three things—
 the script, the script and
 the script."

ALFRED HITCHCOCK
legendary director of *Psycho, Vertigo,
Rear Window* and many others

IT ALL STARTS with the script.

You've probably heard that a thousand times, but it's true. So I'll say it again: It all starts with the script.

For you to have *any* chance of making a standout movie, unless you are an unbelievably genius director—and yes, there is a tiny handful who can spin mediocre scripts into gold statues—but unless you're one of them, you need a standout script.

So, what makes a script stand out?

CONVENTIONAL WISDOM: Study the trades (i.e., *Variety* and *Hollywood Reporter*) and track what is selling. Write something in that genre, with a fresh twist on the formula.

REBEL HEART WISDOM: Write a script with honest, authentic passion. To hell with what is popular or what you think will sell.

The script that stands out is the one that comes from someone's heart. It's the script that is written because the screenwriter loves it, and *has* to write it. It's probably a script that no one else but that particular screenwriter could have written; even if it's an historic epic, it's as personal and specific to the screenwriter as their DNA. It reflects their obsessions, their worldview, their truest loves and values.

If it's written from a place of cynicism (*"Action movies with female leads are hot right now, so I'm writing one of those"*), it will never be great. Trust your heart, tune into your instincts, and write the movie that you would pay to see.

Before we go any further, I want you to do a quick exercise.

The goal here is not to overthink these questions, but to go with the first idea that pops into your mind.

First, I want you to write down ten films you love and would watch right now if you were home alone and they were on TV. These aren't necessarily the movies you claim publicly to be your favorites (because you know your cinephile friends would laugh at you), but these are your own true genuine pleasures, perhaps even guilty ones.

And now I want you to list ten movies you wish you had made. Movies that, when you saw them, hit your envy nerve ("I wish I had thought of that!").

Next, I want you to write down five filmmakers that you love and that you secretly wish you could have their careers. These are the ones that, whether you actually love their movies or not, when you read about them you feel a twinge of envy.

Now, I want you to take some time to study these lists and see what they tell you.

About your first list: Do you see a common thread? Perhaps they are all underdog stories, or tales of true love conquering all? Maybe you see that you're really pretty obsessed with gritty urban dramas, or cop stories? Movies with a positive message, or perhaps even nihilistic horrors? Think about the genres, the story patterns, the kinds of heroes or protagonists they deal with. These are the movies you want to see . . . so, the kind of movie you should be devoting your life to making? It's probably something like these.

The second list can give us an even clearer picture of where our heart lies. This list isn't so much about what entertains you, but what really gets under your skin. Envy is one of our greatest friends in helping us figure out what path we should take. If we wish with all our hearts that we had made a particular movie, it's a pretty strong indicator that it's the kind of movie we should make.

Likewise with filmmakers. Being conscious of the kind of filmmaker that gets your heart beating faster can help you recognize your true aim as an artist. Do you secretly wish you were Kelly Reichardt or Sofia Coppola? The first is the epitome of the intellectual, arty indie filmmaker, the second a far more glamorous and starry type. What do you yearn for as a filmmaker? Do you wish you were Chris Nolan or Richard Linklater or Jim Jarmusch? These are all incredibly successful filmmakers, but they appeal to very different audiences and have very different brands.

The clearer you are about the kind of path you'd ideally like to forge as a filmmaker, the more likely you'll start out making the right film that will help you on that path. Ana Lily Amirpour (director of *A Girl Walks Home Alone at Night* and *The Bad Batch*) once said, "Making a film is like putting on a perfume—you see who it attracts." Make sure you're putting on the right perfume for your big goals. There's no point making a horror film because you think they sell, when really you dream of making romantic comedies.

What if your lists point you in a direction that you didn't totally expect? It's not an uncommon dilemma.

Head says: I want to make a clever art house movie, because they are so impressive and cool.

Heart says: I freaking love vampire movies.

Trust the heart. Every single time. When you are totally in tune with it, success will follow, because you will do your best work.

There is absolutely no point writing something because you think it's the commercially smart thing to do. Forget it. You will never win that race. If you're writing a clever art house thriller because you read in the trades that eight of them sold recently, and one topped the box office last week . . . forget it! Someone else is writing one because they just totally love them, and I guarantee their script will be better than yours.

You are going to do your best work when you are 100% aligned spiritually with the content. So be truthful about where your heart is.

Now you might be thinking, "that's great, but *my* heart . . . ?! It's so freaking uncommercial! None of the really successful movies are about the stuff I really love."

You can stop right there: I made a movie about obsolete technologies, climate change and Buddhist philosophy, complete with dialogue referencing French filmmaker Robert Bresson and the brilliant (but not widely known) German author W. G. Sebald. And you know what? That's *why* the film stood out.

Here's the awesome news: You are not making *Spider-Man*. You do not have to appeal to everyone. Try to do that, and you will screw up any chance you have of making a standout movie.

Instead, be obsessive, be particular, be honest. Be true to your own idiosyncratic, unique, weird loves, and celebrate them. Lean in to the things that genuinely excite you. There are people out there who share those loves, and they will love you forever for giving a voice to them.

The world has enough bland. I often think if you're writing a script and it doesn't scare you in some way, it's not alive. Be bold. Our limitations as writers often correspond with our fears as human beings, so pull up all your courage and face your fears down. Write about the shit that makes you blush. Allow your script to be a strange, vibrant, passionate color that no one has seen before, that scares even you . . . and trust me, if you do that: your screenplay will stand out.

The Importance of *Dérive*

This may seem like a detour, but bear with me, because straying from the main road is often utterly essential for us to do our best creative work. It's easy to get overly focused on the end result of making a film (*Awards! Great reviews! My genius will finally be recognized!*). Nothing wrong with the occasional daydream, but where our attention should really lie is on our daily journey. Sure, there is a destination that we are trying to reach, but the only way we get there is by walking the path, one foot after another, and if we are open-minded on the path, particularly when we are beginning the journey, we'll often find some wonderful and unexpected detours that will raise our work to a whole other standard.

The French Situationists coined a word "*dérive*" (pronounced *de-REEV*), that sums this up. Basically, it's a walk without a goal, a walk that is mapped by your whims; one that allows you to explore a city while being guided by your subconscious. If you are a writer, I invite you to allow yourself to enjoy *dérives* as a way of working. Go to your local library and explore books for no particular reason. Go see a movie that you wouldn't normally go to. Walk in nature, go to a museum, rummage around a thrift store or a flea market. Feed your own curiosity, and let that be the guide of your creativity. The more you can access your own underlying passions, the greater chance you have of writing and developing a truly unique script.

If you do this, will you write a perfect script? There's never any guarantee of that. But you will write a script that is alive, and it will already be better than 90% of the formulaic, dead-in-the-water scripts out there.

EXERCISE

Schedule an hour this week (or longer if you can manage it) to do something out of your ordinary, something you fancy doing *just because*. It can be anything: a walk in a park you've never been to before, an hour of free writing in a café in a different part of town, a visit to a museum you've read about but never visited. The important thing is you take the time to do something that feeds your curiosity and nourishes your artistic self, something that doesn't involve sitting at your computer, gazing at the screen. The activity you choose may not play directly into the script you're dreaming about, but be ready for inspiration in unexpected places.

Four Pillars of a Great Movie

When I was still in high school, my art teacher (shout-out to the wonderful Mr. Richard Caston) introduced me to this Jungian model of art, and over the years it's something I've always come back to. I've realized it's not just true of visual art;

it's also true of movies, and I want to share it with you as yet another method to tune into your heart as it concerns films.

According to this model, all great films (and therefore all great scripts too) have these four elements:

WHY? The story needs to be emotionally engaging—movies need to move people. That's why a lot of us go to the cinema: to laugh, to cry, to empathize, to be scared, to fall in love.

SO WHAT? It needs to be thought provoking—it needs to engage the intellect, and be about more than it seems to be about.

WHAT IF? It needs to be original—an homage is fine, but it is far finer to find your own language. Something fresh in its content, format, and execution.

WHAT? It needs to be well crafted—dialogue needs to ring with elevated truth, and scenes need to be elegant in their start and close.

Truly great films excel in all four of these areas, but many excellent films stand out in just one or two. The films of French auteur Jean Luc Godard, for example, are incredibly original and very thought provoking, but arguably don't engage us emotionally to quite the same extent. Most Hollywood studio films get ten out of ten for being well crafted—they are technically excellent—but originality is often not their strong suit (see a million remakes and sequels if you doubt me).

EXERCISE

Write down answers to these questions:

1   Go back to the lists of the movies you love. Do they tend to favor one pillar over another? What is most important to you? What REALLY excites you in a film?

2   Do you tend to lean towards one of these pillars over others? It's normal. Which is it?

3   Is there a way to develop your work so it satisfies another one of these pillars? It's worth considering that even movies with one singular aim (i.e., a horror movie aims to scare people, a comedy to make them laugh) will be better if they also satisfy another pillar (for example, they also make you think or they are original in the way they are constructed). The stronger your pillars are, the better your script will be—thus the better your movie!

When is my script ready?

There comes a time for every writer when they wonder if their script is ready to share with others. You've completed a first draft. You're excited and raring to go! I get it—I've been there.

The first thing to know: Don't be impatient. When working on a script with no external deadline or delivery date, time is on your side. Use it!

The better your script is when you first share it with potential cast and crew, the greater chance you have of attracting real talents to work with you—and you're going to need those gifted folk to make an awesome movie. The more talented they are, the better shot you have of making a standout film. So before you give it to anyone you possibly want to work with, make sure you're giving them the strongest version of your script.

Also, it's crucial that you never share a script with

possible financiers until you've prepared a whole package, which includes the best version of your script. You can't go back to people twice, or ask them to read other drafts of your screenplay. It won't happen. People are far too busy, so you need to make sure that, when you get to that stage, you are seriously putting your best foot forward.

It's worth noting that script development time is cheap compared to other stages of making a film. You can afford extra days and weeks. It doesn't cost a nickel, so allow yourself that luxury. After you finish your first draft, put it away for a month, then come back to it with fresh eyes. That usually helps you see what you need to change. Make the changes you want, And then, if you feel like there's really nothing more you can do to it to make it better, get ready to share it.

At this point, you don't want to share the script with anyone you might want to ask to work on it. You want to share it only with people that I call "feedback friends"; people who will take the time to read it, and share their very honest thoughts about it, so that you can make it better.

Please don't just share it with your mom, or other people who adore you, and who will say nothing bad about your work—although feel free to start with someone like that if you need a confidence boost. I always share my scripts first with my husband, Chris, because he always thinks my work is awesome, and helps me silence the crazy loud voice of doubt. I know I won't get hard criticism from him, but he gives me the courage I need to hit SEND to tougher readers. At that point, I usually share it with two or three more feedback friends who are worth their weight in gold, and who have been cultivated over the years. These are people who basically dig my work and my voice, but who aren't afraid to be fiercely honest with me.

So, what makes a good feedback friend?

Good feedback isn't just opinions (i.e., "I hate this story, I don't like films about road trips, movies with free-spirited girls suck, they're so cliché," etc).

Rather, good feedback goes like this: "It seems to me that these are your aims . . . here's where it works . . . But here's where, for me, it's not quite there or could be stronger."

In essence, a good feedback friend seeks to understand what the writer is aiming for and helps them achieve it. They're not trying to impose their opinion or their vision of what the script should be. They're really trying to see the film as you see it, but are objective enough that they can help you see what isn't working. Being a good feedback friend is a skill that you should develop yourself, so you can be one to others.

Typically I recommend seeking feedback from two to five different people, depending how clear you feel about what you need to do to progress. They don't need to be screenwriters or people in the industry (though sharing it with other industry people can definitely help because they are used to reading screenplays and the format won't put them off). You may also want to get one person to read it who you think is the ideal audience member for your film.

After they've read your script, take them out for a coffee and have a chat with them about it. In addition to asking them their overall feeling about the piece, I tend to always ask a few of the same questions:

1. **Did you understand everything? Was there anything that you didn't get? Anything that was confusing?**
Unless you're making *Mulholland Drive*, it's essential that the plot is clear and that no one gets lost or confused. Sometimes as the writer, you don't realize that some crucial piece of information is missing, so this is essential to find out.

2. **Were you ever bored? If so, when?**
A script can be many things, but the one thing it should NEVER be is boring. Ask them what page they were on when they put it down. Ideally, they'll say they read it in a oner. Otherwise there's still work to do.

3. **Did you believe the main characters? Was there anything that struck you as false, or made you say "They'd never do that!"?**
I don't really care if people "like" the main characters, but I do care that they believe and engage with them. If that's not happening, then there is a major problem, and it's back to the drawing board.

You might also have some very specific questions, things you're grappling with in the script at that moment. For example, you might be wondering if you need to include more of a character's backstory, or whether a central plot point is believable. Ask your feedback friend every question that is bugging you in any way. This is a golden opportunity to take your script to the next level.

As you gather feedback: if more than one person says the same thing ("I got bored around page 40," "I didn't buy that he would call his dad there"), you've got a problem, and it's worth dealing with it now. Even if you don't see it—if *everyone* else tells you it's a problem, believe them. It's a problem. As a friend of mine once said, "If fifty Russians tell you you're drunk, you're drunk." Don't fight it. Remember, it's much easier to fix it now than to wait until you've shot a film, and you're running up against the same issue with the edit.

If, on the other hand, only one person calls you to task on something, trust your own instinct. If their problem with your script lands with you, and you feel in your heart that they're right, change it. If you don't, then don't. It's your script, and you should feel confident about your choices. Sometimes that means standing your ground.

A final word about receiving feedback

This isn't always easy, but always try to listen to feedback with an open heart, and a genuine willingness to learn.

Set your ego aside. This is not about you. It's about your work.

And trust me, I know: It's not always easy to separate the two, and it's never easy hearing someone say that they didn't like something you wrote, but it's truly a gift they are giving you at this stage.

It's a gift that they took the time to read your work and to talk to you about it, and it's a gift if they are honest and willing to voice their negatives as well as their positives. So be brave, and accept that gift with grace. Don't get defensive, and don't argue with them. Try to really understand what they are saying. If they're telling you something you strongly disagree with, bite your tongue and let it pass.

However, it's important that you trust your instincts. Occasionally we'll give our work to someone who sabotages it. They'll tell you every single thing that's wrong with it, and you'll leave them feeling depressed, like you'll never write again. Trust me—I've experienced it. The thing about that person: They are not a feedback friend. Their negativity is not about your script; it's about them.

At this early stage of development, your script is like a tiny, green shoot of a baby plant; it's very easy to kill. Your job is to protect it and nourish it, so that it can grow into a big healthy tree, at which point bitter armchair critics can take axes to it (and sadly in most cases, they will . . .), but by then it will survive (and so will you). A baby script can be crushed so easily though—so don't let it happen. If you have the misfortune of that experience, just whisk your baby away from them and give it tons of water and love (give yourself the same). Do what you can to erase their negativity from your mind and NEVER share your work with them again. Lesson learned!

Once you have gathered feedback, work on your script some more. Afterwards, if you still don't feel 100% about it, share it with a few more people until you really feel you've nailed it.

Yay! I think my script is ready!

CONVENTIONAL WISDOM: Keep working, keep working: rewrite, rewrite, rewrite.

REBEL HEART WAY: Don't overcook it. If you're generally getting good feedback; if you feel you've flushed it out and it's expressing well what you want—then pull the trigger and move to the next step.

One last word before you do:

Overdeveloping can definitely be a problem. Our first instincts are often our best.

But: Underdeveloping can also be a problem, so really try to be honest with yourself.

In the spirit of honesty

There are many flaws in my first film, and most of them I can live with—because I know why they're there. They're connected with budget constraints or tech difficulties that we were having on the shoot: things totally out of my control. But the things that kill me—destroy me on every viewing— are things that even at the script stage I knew weren't right, but somehow thought, "Oh, it's good enough." Dialogue that I knew wasn't there, entire scenes that weren't everything they should be.

And I think, "Wow. Why didn't I keep working on it? Why didn't I push myself to get it right on the page?" And it's just one or two scenes, but it's definitely a mistake I wouldn't make again. I made it already so you don't have to. If in your heart you feel it's not the best you can do, keep working on it. Don't give up.

But what if I'm not a writer?!

Almost everything we've covered so far still applies. As a producer or director of the film, the more you are guided by your heart and your passions, the more likely you are to succeed.

You will likely fall into one of two categories:

- You have a story that you want to make into a film, and you need to find a writer to write the script.

- You just want to make a movie, and you're open to finding a great script.

If you are in the first category, there are a number of ways of going about this.

CONVENTIONAL WAY: You pay a fairly inexperienced writer $5000 or less (I've heard of people paying as little as $2000) for a first draft.

For this amount of money, you will own all the rights to the script, but do make sure that you have a contract that makes clear they have given up all rights, so there are no issues further down the line. At this level of payment, be warned! You might get lucky and find a genuinely talented screenwriter who is just starting out—but you might also get a script that is simply unusable. I've seen it before—and even though the script was relatively inexpensive (Note: If you hired an experienced writer who was covered by the Writer's Guild agreement, you'd pay upwards of $60,000 for a first draft), it's money down the drain if the script is no good.

REBEL HEART WAY: You find a writer who is as excited about your idea as you are. This might take time. This might mean meeting a lot of writers. But you find someone who gets excited by your story, and who wants to write it as much as you want to tell it. They are motivated less by a modest paycheck, and more by the passion to tell that story.

As you are not paying them upfront, you will be tied together on the project, so make sure they are really the right person; that they not only "get" your idea, but that they have the necessary experience and talent to do a good job with it. Read a script that they have written, and make sure that you love their writing.

Even in this perfect case where you adore each other and are BFFs, it is worth having a contract that makes clear what the deal is, and that allows the possibility for you to buy them out. It's kind of like having a prenup, and although it's not romantic, it will save you from trauma later if you decide you need to go your separate ways.

So, where do I find a writer?

There are a million ways to do this, but here are a few ideas to get you started:

- Reach out to established writers of movies you admire (though only do this if they are working a level accessible to you, i.e., probably low budget indies).

- Scour the Blacklist (a list of popular unproduced screenplays, usually by up-and-coming screenwriters) for similar projects, and reach out to the writers.

- Look at who's been selected for the Sundance writer's lab, or Film Independent's, and nab an up-and-comer.

- Reach out to your local film school.

- Put an ad on Craigslist (Ha! You think I'm joking . . . but you'll learn, I'm really not!).

- Find out about screenwriters' meet ups in your town (check online) and attend one.

There are a thousand ways—and trust me, there are thousands of writers out there; your job is to find the right one who shares your passions and your hopes for making the same kind of movie.

Once you find the writer, the process is much the same as if you were writing it yourself. Don't proceed any further until you absolutely *love* the script for your film and you are utterly convinced that it is the best it can be. Don't settle for anything less than a screenplay you feel passionately excited about and are desperate to share with the world.

STEP 1 CHECK LIST

☐ Write your script (or have it written for you).

☐ Share it and get feedback.

☐ Hone it until it's so freaking awesome you are insanely desperate to share it with the world.

☐ Be grateful for the journey you're on, and celebrate that you've got a brilliant script.

STEP 2
SET A
START DATE

"You create your
opportunities by
asking for them."

SHAKTI GAWAIN
proponent of creative visualization, wise woman

SO YOU'VE DECIDED your script is ready. What next?

CONVENTIONAL PATH: Send it to agents, production companies and talent, hoping someone else will love it too.

REBEL HEART WAY: Set a start date.

This might seem crazy. Set a start date? Doesn't that happen after you raise the money?

No. You must do it right now. It's the secret key to making your film a reality rather than another elusive dream.

Without a doubt, one of the hardest things about making a film is getting it started. It's that initial momentum that's really hard to come by.

Ever heard of Newton's *First Law of Motion*?

> Every object in a state of uniform motion tends to remain in that state of motion unless an external force is applied to it.

Your film is the object, and at this point, it's not moving. You are the external force, and to get the film moving, it's going to take a lot of power. Setting a start date will initiate that magic, life-giving force in a way that will blow your mind. Why? Two reasons: The first is a woo-woo, hippie, "if you visualize it, it will happen" reason, and the other is a far more pragmatic, non-negotiable, material world reason. Take your pick if you need to know the why, but honestly both are true.

Let's talk about the real-world reason first, just in case you are skeptical of woo-woo (and who can blame you?!).

Let's imagine that you set your date six months from now, on April 2 or November 7 or whatever it is, and you put it in your calendar and start saying to people, "On that date we are going to start shooting."

The first effect of this is that you now have a very clear, tangible goal. What do you have to do every day from now until then to make it happen? You start to feel a real sense of urgency, the type that arises when you have a deadline (ask any writer about this). You have to hold yourself accountable and you have to make it happen, no matter what. It's no longer, "It will happen when we get what we need"; it's now, "We have to get what we need now, so it will happen"—and the difference between those mindsets is exactly what you need to make it real.

Another very powerful effect is that, when you tell other people you are making a movie, it's no longer "one day," or "when we get the money," which always sounds like a pipe dream. It's firm, it's going to happen, it's concrete—and this is not only great for you psychologically, it's also great for people you are trying to convince to join your team (whether as financiers or creative partners).

Nothing is more appealing to people than something that actually feels like it's happening. They want to jump on board! There's a clear plan, this thing is happening with or without them. They won't want to miss out. They will take you more seriously, and you are far more likely to close the deal with them.

I often think that getting a film started is an issue of faking it until it's real. The more you act like it's absolutely, definitely,

100% happening, the more likely it is to become real. If you have doubts, if it's a cloudy dream and even you're not convinced that it will happen, forget it already.

So here's the woo-woo that I happen to believe is totally true: The clearer you are about your dreams, the more likely they are to come true. If you are vague and imprecise about what you want, you are very unlikely to get it. A magic force will ignite when you write in your calendar that your shoot will start on a particular day. So get clear, get focused, be brave, and set your start date now.

You can do it!

So, when should your start date be?

If literally all you've got is your script and a dream, (i.e., you have no finance at all, no budget, no crew, no locations), the absolute minimum is seven months away, though longer is probably smarter.

Realistically, it's going to take at least four months to get your package together to raise finance. Then, it will be at least two months of going after the money and getting it in your bank. Finally, you're going to need a solid four weeks of pre-production. So that's seven months.

Of course, other things might play into how you choose your start date. With my first film, I wanted to shoot in Death Valley, and there were only certain months of the year that it was feasible (summer not possible unless we wanted to die from heat exposure). So in September, I set the start date as April 3rd of the following year. Definitely think about the subject matter of your film, and what time of year provides the ideal lighting for your shoot. You might find you are aiming for as much as 12 months away.

Now of course, you may not make your start date, and that's okay.

I didn't make mine that first time, but we started shooting a few weeks later, which still was nothing short of a miracle.

The important thing is that you have a clear, pronounced goal that you can share with others who might work with you. You have a precise intention on which you can act, and not just a fuzzy dream. Guaranteed, that is what you need to make this dream of yours come true.

STEP 2 CHECKLIST

- ☐ Set a start date.
- ☐ Write it in your calendar.
- ☐ Start telling everyone that you will start to shoot your movie on that day. You have to make it happen now, no turning back.
- ☐ Be grateful for the journey you are on, and celebrate that you've got a clear plan.

STEP 3
FIND A LINE
PRODUCER

"It takes two flints to
make a fire."

LOUISA MAY ALCOTT
author of *Little Women*

NOW THAT YOU have set a date, you need to start getting into action. No more excuses. You have to hold yourself accountable, and you have to make shit happen. So how do you begin to do that?

First up: You need to find a line producer.

The line producer, sometimes nicknamed a "nuts and bolts producer" is the person who will break down your script, make a schedule and a budget based on it, and manage your production financially. They will also be responsible for hiring your below-the-line crew (i.e., everyone except for heads of departments), and deal with contracts. You could call them the business manager of your film, and also the human resources manager. They are in charge of all the day-to-day logistics of making your movie. In other words, this person is very, very important to you.

You might wonder: Why do you need one now? Shouldn't you be going after finance, and *then* hire one?

CONVENTIONAL WISDOM: Attach talent and start raising money now.

REBEL HEART WAY: Create a compelling, bulletproof package before you try to raise money.

Before you consider raising finance, you really want to get your ducks in a row.

Don't just have a phenomenal script.

Have a well thought-out **budget** that shows exactly how much you need and how you will spend every dollar.

Have a **schedule** that backs your budget up and shows that the budget is realistic.

Have a **business plan** that shows you understand the film marketplace and have a clear vision of how to recoup your investors' money.

There are creative ducks to line up too, but they'll come later. Right now, you need a budget and schedule, and unless you are a line producer yourself, this is not something you should attempt alone. It will take you forever, and it won't be reliable. You need someone who knows the real market costs of every aspect of making a film in your city; someone who has contacts within the industry, and who understands the reality of making a film on a very tight budget.

So, how do you find one?

First, look at films that you admire, shot in your city, that have a similar budget (if there are any). Find out who line-produced them, and reach out to them.

Ask friends in the film business for a personal recommendation. Also try your social media network, and ask around on Facebook or Twitter.

Reach out to your local film school, and ask if there is anyone who might be interested.

Finally, if you are in a big city with a lot of film people (particularly LA or NYC), consider putting an ad on Craigslist.

I know what you're thinking—and it's probably something to do with Craigslist killers you've heard about and the *Casual Encounters* section. But seriously, I've personally had huge success with this approach. Through Craigslist, I not only met the person who became my line producer (and great friend forever), I also met my editor (who has edited all three of my films). It's possible!

The key to success with a Craigslist ad is to be very specific about who you are and what you are looking for. Don't be generic. Let your personality shine through so that it will attract truly like-minded souls. And never lie! It sounds obvious, but there's no point making it sound like a paid gig if it isn't.

A word on that: Do you have to pay a line producer to make your budget and schedule? In most cases, I am all about people getting paid to work on your movie. I'm not a fan of getting people to work for free (much more on this later). However, I do think it's okay to ask people to defer payment until you have money coming in. So in this case, I think it's fine to ask someone to create a budget so that you can raise money, and then they'll be paid. You have invested hundreds of unpaid hours at this point, so I don't think it's wrong to ask someone to invest a few.

Just be very clear about the fact you are offering deferred payment. Some experienced line producers do expect money up front (probably around $1000-$2000). But there are people out there, usually up-and-comers, who will do it for deferred pay, especially if they get excited about the project and believe it could be a winner.

To give you an idea of what a Craigslist ad might look like, here's what our ad said, for real:

LINE PRODUCER NEEDED
FOR MICRO BUDGET INDIE MOVIE

We're looking for a line producer to help prepare
budgets and schedules on an ultra low budget indie
feature, scheduled to shoot April 2009*.

We need someone who understands the realities of making a movie on a shoestring, and knows how to budget
accordingly.

We've already got a committed group of SAG actors and
an experienced crew**, and we want this to be a fun
and inspiring experience for everyone involved.

You might be a recent film-school grad, or an experienced line producer or production coordinator/super-
visor who'd love to work on something with this kind
of passion and heart—to work with a group of people
who are doing it because they love the project, and
they truly believe they can make a real gem of a movie.

There will be deferred payment, and of course, you'll
get a credit on a feature—but the main reason to get
involved is because you get excited about this and
want to be a part of it.

If you love movies like Before Sunrise, Annie Hall,
Pierrot Le Fou and Stranger Than Paradise...well,
you'll know where we're coming from.

So if this strikes a chord with you and you'd like
more information, send me an email and tell me a bit
about yourself, and we can take it from there.

We look forward to hearing from you!

. . . .

* You see how that start date works?! It makes the film seem like it's really happening, even though I had
no idea when I was writing this ad exactly how I would make it happen by then.

** To be totally honest, I think we had Chris (my husband, who is a SAG actor), and one other guy
possibly attached as an actor, and crew?! I think that was Chris, my husband again! But stretching the
truth to make something sound solid is okay, as long as it's grounded in facts.

From our ad, I heard from around 50 people (it was in LA), and out of those I met with about 15. Some were very experienced, some not so much. Some seemed super smart, others super enthusiastic.

At the end of the day, I believe enthusiasm and "clicking" are far more important than experience. If someone is really keen to work with you, and has the basic level of ability for their job, but they simply don't have a ton of experience, this person is gold. They are a far better hire than someone who's done the job a thousand times and is only doing it because they need the (deferred) paycheck.

It's worth considering too that if someone is used to working with bigger budgets (i.e., they work regularly in TV), they don't really know how to budget for a tiny movie. They literally can't do it. They can't think out of the box. I met one guy who told me it was flat out impossible to make my film for less than a million bucks. I just smiled at him and thanked him for his time.

For the record, once our film (which was made for less than $140,000) had been selected for Sundance, that same guy emailed me and said: *"I'll never say impossible again."* Which is something we should all agree on: Everything is possible, including finding a line producer who will do the job for no money up front, and who will create a budget and schedule that work for your goals.

Now let's boil down the essential qualities of a line producer:

1. **Knows real costs of making a film in your area**
   This is non-negotiable. If they don't know this, you
   might as well make the budget yourself—and note
   that I said "in your area." If they are LA based and you
   want to make your movie in North Dakota, unless they
   have experience there, forget it. You need someone
   who knows the costs of local equipment hires, insurance, crew payments, as well as location fees. Check
   that they have at least one credit, even if it's a student
   film. In your conversation, hit them with a ballpark of
   what you want the total budget to be and listen to their
   reaction.

2. **Knows union rules and how to navigate them**
   If you're in LA or NY in particular this is very important. You need someone who knows the rules and will
   not let you get into trouble. Ask them if they've dealt
   with unions before, and what they think the best strategy for your film is.

3. **Has a "can do" attitude; is a natural problem solver**
   On a microbudget film, you need a person who can
   think out of the box to get shit done, because you
   won't be able to throw money at problems. It helps
   if the line producer has a positive attitude towards
   problems, and is willing and able to work in a flexible
   way to achieve your goals. Working with someone who

consistently shakes their head and says "no" more than "let's figure it out" will be soul-destroying for you and everyone else working on the film.

4. **Has an understanding of how to schedule for success**

A solid schedule is essential for the success of your film. There's much more about this in the next chapter, but for now, make sure you ask your potential line producer about their experience of scheduling. Make sure that, at the very least, they will be realistic about the number of days you will need to shoot.

5. **Understands the value of putting the money on the screen**

With microbudget films, every dollar needs to be on screen. Sure everyone gets paid, but make sure they understand that there won't be big paychecks for above-the-line cast and crew (line producer's fee included).

6. **Knows great crew**

They will be doing the hiring of the crew, so if they know a bunch of people, it's unbelievably helpful.

7. **Has a great sense of humor**

This is a no-brainer, and should be a necessity for every crewmember! You want to be surrounded by people you can laugh with. Making a film is hard enough; don't make it harder by doing it with stress machines, no matter how fancy their resume is.

8. **Is great with people**

   The line producer is like the human resources agent in your film, and to keep everyone happy in your cast and crew, it really helps if they are positive and upbeat in their attitude. All the heads of departments will be begging your line producer for more money (it's the nature of making a film), and your line producer is the one who'll have to keep saying "no" to them. Make sure that they're the kind of person who makes "no" a sweet pill to swallow, not an angry one! The happier your crew, the better shot you have of making a great film. The energy of your line producer will set the tone. Make it a good one.

One last word: When you are hiring anyone to work with you, *trust your instincts*. Do you like this person? Do you trust them? Do you feel at ease with them? Do you laugh together? Do you think they understand the kind of film you want to make? Do they love it as much as you? For me, these things are super important, far more so than whether they've done tons of movies before.

You are creating art together, not going to war. Surround yourself with people who inspire you and fill you with courage and excitement. Don't worry if they don't have a ton of experience—you don't either! Think of it as if you are forming a rock band: You're all starting from the same place, but with the right chemistry, and a shared vision, anything is possible.

Once you decide on that person, and they accept the job, congratulations! You are seriously on your way to making your movie. It's no longer just you striving to make it happen; you have the beginning of a team—and the more people who become involved, the stronger the force for making your film will be. Soon you will be unstoppable.

STEP 3 CHECKLIST

☐ Contact potential line producers.

☐ Meet them.

☐ Choose one.

☐ Be grateful for the journey you are on, and celebrate the fact that you are no longer the only one on the team!

STEP 4
LOCK DOWN A SCHEDULE AND BUDGET

"The enemy of art is the absence of limitations"

ORSON WELLES
genius filmmaker and actor, director
of *Citizen Kane, A Touch of Evil*

THIS IS A huge step, and one that will probably take some time to get right. The reality of how you are going to make your film kicks in, and, if you do it right, you create a solid blueprint for the success of your film.

Let's be very clear about one thing: If you don't budget and schedule well, you have no chance of making a good movie. Literally zero. Many movies have been doomed before they even started shooting, because either the budget wasn't realistic or the schedule was over-ambitious. Without a proper budget and schedule, you haven't got a chance, so it's really worth taking the time to create a plan that works.

Obviously, it's not you who is going to make the budget and schedule. Your line producer is going to do it—that's why you found them in the last step. But nonetheless, you will work with them to achieve your goals, and it's crucial that you have some understanding of budgeting and scheduling so that you can ensure that they create a realistic foundation on which to build your film.

There are basically two ways to make a budget:

CONVENTIONAL WAY: You write down the market costs of all the things you'll need to make the film (i.e., the salaries of all the workers, the cost of hiring the essential equipment, the price of feeding your cast and crew, etc.), then you add these all together and bingo; there's the cost of your film.

REBEL HEART WAY: You have a number in mind (i.e., $100K) and you figure out how you can juggle all the other numbers so that they add up to that amount.

The conventional way generally leads to a stratospheric sum that you'll never be able to raise. This leads to depression and the belief that you'll never be able to make your freaking film. The second way allows you to make a budget for a sum that makes sense for you. You'll feel empowered and certain that you'll make your movie.

Now, the question arises: If you're going to take the second strategy, why would you pick $100,000 rather than $50,000 or $200,000, or indeed $500,000?

You might start by thinking about what you can get your hands on. Certainly that's what I did with *Obselidia*. I knew of a potential investor who claimed to have $100,000 to put in a movie. I wanted my film to be that movie, so I wanted to show that not only did I have a great script, but also that I could pull it off for that amount of money.

I also consciously felt that I did not want the burden and pressure of a higher budget. It was my first film. I wanted to know where every penny was being spent. I wanted to know what every crewmember was doing. I wanted total creative freedom. And I wanted the film to be small enough that if it failed completely, as it had the very good chance to do, it wouldn't be noticed.

Some of us think about how much we can realistically get hold of, but others think they should aim to get the most they can. These people often subscribe to the idea that the bigger your budget, the more you are making a legitimate film; the idea that somehow a million dollar movie is more of a movie than one made for a tenth of that. I'd like to call bullshit on that. The process is the same however much it costs, and the ultimate value of the film has nothing to do with its price.

I don't want to dim anyone's dreams, but I'm going to suggest you think of this in another way, particularly if this is your first film and you are planning to make it off the grid, raising the cash yourself.

The question you should be asking is this: How much can we hope to make from this film? And then get real about it.

I know in business plans for their projects, filmmakers tend to highlight the rare cases of movies that have done out of the park, awesome business. That's why in business plans for tiny indie movies, you always see *The Blair Witch Project, Pulp Fiction, Once,* and *My Big Fat Greek Wedding.* Movies that were made for relatively little money, but grossed megabucks.

Reality check: It's highly unlikely (to say the very least) that your movie is going to be a phenomenon like one of those. It *might* be (never say impossible, remember?), but building your career plan on winning the lottery is not a smart strategy. You want to create a situation whereby even if your film isn't that one-in-ten-million hit, you still get to make another one. And how do you do that? You make your money back.

So now's the time to do your research. Find out a realistic goal of return for your film by educating yourself on what other films make. This isn't as easy as it should be, because the film industry is full of lies when it comes down to how much money films actually made. Everyone wants to appear successful, so they don't release the real numbers for distribution deals or money raised through digital streaming.

I'm going to share a few with you right now about my film *Obselidia*, which might surprise you. For one year of licensing on Netflix, we received $6,000 (and I've been told by other indie filmmakers that this was high; some I know received only $2,000 for that honor). After the aggregator took their share, we received a check for less than $4,000. From Amazon and iTunes, we received checks for hundreds of dollars, not thousands. Our biggest single check was for $25,000, which was a buy out for airline and cruise ship rights.

Could we have done better financially with the movie if we had released it in a different way and been more savvy? Absolutely. But please don't delude yourself into thinking that you are going to make hundreds of thousands of dollars for a quirky indie drama with no stars, unless you get incredibly, insanely, one-in-a-zillion lucky.

Speaking of delusions, don't assume that you will make your movie, take it to a festival and sell it for millions. More than likely, that is not going to happen. You might get it into festivals, you might not. Even if you do make it to a major festival (and the odds are already hugely stacked against you there), there's no guarantee you'll sell it.

Even if you do sell it, the distribution deals you are offered might look very different from what you imagine. I know a lot of filmmakers, and they have privately told me the truth of what their films sold for. Here's the thing: Everyone wants to look successful, so outwardly, they make it seem great regardless of how much it actually made. They announce in the trades that they got distribution (sometimes not mentioning what the deal was worth, sometimes quoting a wildly inflated figure). They add it to their IMDb page, brag about it at dinner parties, and the fact they got distribution validates them and their work.

But guess how much they often get paid for giving up the rights to their films?

ZERO.

That's right. Not a freaking penny. You might be shocked by this, and you have every right to be. After all, the filmmakers and their investors took the big risks, and surely they should be compensated for that upfront. In a fair world, where hardly any movies were made, that would be the case, but the market you're entering is totally overflowing with content, so it's not easy to sell.

We'll have an in-depth discussion about all of this later, when we talk about distribution, monetization, and making smart choices, but the reason I'm bringing it up here is this:

You cannot start to budget your film unless you have an idea of how you're going to sell it at the end.

Reality check: Without money you can't make a film, and if you need to raise money, in actual fact, you're not just making a film, you're starting a business. It's incredibly important that you embrace the business aspect from the beginning. Doing this is what is going to make you a success and enable you to pursue your art over the years.

Like with any business, before you start producing something, you look at the market, figure out how much you can get for your product, and budget your expenses to produce accordingly. There is no point making a t-shirt for ten bucks if you can only sell it for five. If you can sell it for five, you've got to figure out a way to make it for three or four (or even better, fifty cents!).

So before you do your budget, do your research. Make a list of films that are similar to yours, and be very clear about what that would look like. Your film might be just like *Little Miss Sunshine* in tone and theme, but unless you have stars like Greg Kinnear and Toni Collette in it, it's not really comparable. Try to find films with budgets that resemble your own.

Now you need to find out how much these films made. It's not the easiest question to answer, because revenue from digital streaming and DVD sales is not made public, and filmmakers are often less than honest, because they want to appear more successful than they are. So how do you find out?

I suggest you personally reach out to filmmakers with genuinely comparable movies to yours, and ask them to share the truth of what they made from their movies. Tell them it's confidential, that you won't share it anywhere, and that it's purely for your own research. Some will spill the beans; some won't. I think it's crazy when filmmakers won't be honest with each other though, because the only way we can win this game is if we share honest experiences with each other.

Other ways to research: Dig into the resources of Film Collaborative, who are trying to create more transparency around distribution; although a little old, read Ted Hope's blog page (Hope for Film), and Google "DIY online distribution" to get the latest news and numbers. *Filmmaker* magazine and Moviemaker.com are also good resources for up-to-date information. Increasingly, indie filmmakers are realizing how important it is to share this information with one another, and more are having the courage to do it.

Once you have done this, start creating a plan to sell your film, monetize your work, and repay your investors. This will involve identifying your target audience and how you will reach them.

Seriously: Don't wait until you've finished your movie to figure out who's going to watch it.

Have an idea of the business you think your film can do, couple that with how much money you think you can realistically raise, and ask your line producer to create a budget for that amount.

How much is enough?

You might still be wondering, how much do I *need* to make my movie?

Obviously it depends on the film. You're not going to make a period piece, or an action film, or a film with a ton of VFX on a shoestring budget, but if you have a contemporary, character-driven piece, it's possible to do it for a tiny amount. Literally for the cost of an iPhone camera.

However, if you really want it to make an impression (with all technical elements executed at a professional level) as a movie that can hold its own in any festival or any theater screen, it's hard to do it for less than $100,000.

I'm not saying it's impossible to do it for less. Countless examples prove me wrong there.

But at less than $100,000, some people are not going to be paid, so it's harder to get a professional crew, enormous favors are going to have to happen, and furthermore it will be very difficult to have a good sound mix or color correction. In a nutshell, you will risk compromising the quality of the film's technical aspects.

With a budget of less than $50,000, this is even more true.

Yes, we've all heard of *El Mariachi*, the $7,000 movie, but hopefully we've also heard how the studio spent millions on it to make it look and sound like the movie that was eventually released.

You'll often hear filmmakers at festivals brag about their tiny budgets. They wear it like a badge of honor: "You spent $50,000? Ha! We made ours for only $10,000!" When you think about it, what they are bragging about is that no one who worked on their movie got paid—and what's cool about that? If people are going to show up to work on your film, and give you their best day after day, then they should get bucks for it. It obviously won't be top dollar when you're on a tight budget, but $100 per day for most crewmembers is a good place to start.

On this note, you should get paid too! I've never met a post sound mixer who will work for free—why should you? Don't think of your filmmaking as an expensive hobby; this is your job, and the sooner you think of it like that, the sooner you will make money at it and appreciate your own value. So please don't aim to make your budget insanely super low. Instead, aim for a realistic amount that will value your time and energy, as well as the time of your crew.

Of course, you can get incredibly creative with how to stretch your money, and make something fabulous on a shoestring. I know one filmmaker who made a movie for $64,000 that looked awesome and everyone got paid. How did she do it? By shooting one weekend a month for eleven months, thereby halving her camera rental costs. Anything's possible.

But the fact is, even as you try to drive your budget ever lower, there are certain elements that cost money, and they are unavoidable if you want your film to have a shot at really standing out. If you look at the nominees for the Cassavetes Award at the Independent Spirit Awards (an award given to movies with a budget of less than $500,000), you'll find that most of them are in the $150,000–$300,000 range. Very rarely will there be one for less than that.

With $150,000 you can make a great film that can stand up to anything, a film that looks and sounds as good as a studio movie; a film where viewers won't complain, "clearly they had no money!"

Look at the fantastic *Blue Ruin* as an example of this. Made for under $300,000, it makes most thrillers made with 100 times that budget look tired. I doubt that, even if the filmmakers had had a bigger budget, the film would have been any better. It just would have star names in it.

If your budget is more than $300,000, unless you have meaningful star names attached or a really special hook, you are probably budgeting too high. It will be very hard, if not impossible, to make your money back, and that could make it more difficult for you to make further films in the future. Remember: the aim is not just to make one killer film, but also to have a career where you get to make many!

The schedule

Your budget is going to be very dependent upon your schedule. Typically the line producer will do the schedule breakdown first, so they can see how many days of filming it's going to take to make your film, and that will be basis for the cost.

These days it's common to shoot an indie film in around eighteen days; my first film was done in eighteen, my second film, despite having ten times the budget, only had nineteen days.

Let's be honest about something: Eighteen days to shoot a movie is short and it's hard. If your script has 100 pages, you're looking at an average of 5.5 pages a day. That's a lot.

But to have more days, your costs will shoot up. You'll pay more wages, incur longer rental fees, and have more locations fees. Shooting days are expensive. It's simple economics. The shoot is probably going to be the most expensive period of your filmmaking experience, so keeping it short saves money.

Still, the desire and need to keep it short for financial reasons must be balanced against having enough time to do the script justice. There's no point agreeing to a schedule that, from the start, looks like *"we'll get this if we're lucky."* You have to feel confident that, not only will you make each day (i.e., shoot everything on the schedule), but that you'll have time to do it well.

This can't be emphasized enough:

Make sure that your film is truly doable on your schedule.

If your line producer comes back with a schedule in which the average is six pages a day, or there is regularly one company move (or more) per day (i.e., shooting more than one location per day), unless you have a very specific, smart strategy of how to make that work, don't even think about it. You won't be able to make a great film in those circumstances.

Five-and-a-half pages a day is hard; personally, I dream of a situation where the average is no more than four. You kill your chances of making a good film if you don't. And remember: you're not just trying to make a movie; you're trying to make one that has the chance to stand out.

So, if your script is 100 pages, and you know that you can't afford more than 18 days, what do you do?

Time to cut pages from the script.

And I can hear you screaming, *"But my script is perfect, I need every page!"*

You don't. Trust me. If you don't cut them now, you'll cut them in editing. Guaranteed. Far better to do it now at this stage, and give yourself time to shoot the scenes you'll definitely need, and shoot them well, instead of busting your ass to shoot footage that will end up in the trash—and find that the footage you *really* need just isn't good enough.

If you are 100% sure that you need *every* page of your script, that there's no "repeat beats" (i.e., moments that repeat what has come before), that everything is as tight as it can be, that every scene is either forwarding the story or revealing something new and essential about the characters, then accept that you need to schedule more days, and find a way to raise that extra money for the budget. Do not risk compromising the quality of the film because you simply don't have the time to do it justice. It's not worth it.

When you start digging into your schedule, you also start getting real about your locations.

Something that can kill a film faster than anything is having too many locations and company moves. You are not giving your film the chance to be great if you load up on too many locations because it is expensive to have too many, and all the time spent moving from one location to the next loses you shooting time. It easily takes two hours to leave one location, pack up, then set up at another, even if they don't require a long travel time in between. Losing two hours out of your twelve-hour day? It kills you. If you do it every day for a week, it's the equivalent of losing a day. So do the smart thing, and minimize your locations.

Often, this means thinking creatively about your scenes. Do the characters really need to sit in a café to drink coffee at the end of their date? Cafes are typically hard to get, expensive, and require a lot of extras to make them seem real. Perhaps they could drink coffee at one of their homes (if that is where a lot of the action takes place)? Look at all your locations and ask: What happens in the scene? Does it have to take place in this location? If it is essential, keep it. But if it's not, cut it.

Another tactic involves the illusions of movie magic. Could you use one location for multiple purposes? For example, if you rent one large house as a key location, could you use two rooms to be one character's home, and one room as another character's office? Audiences will never know! Thinking like this can save you a lot of time and money—and that's what will enable you to make a great film for less.

Setting a rhythm

Once you've decided how many days you will need to shoot, you start the fun process of really figuring out how to get the most out of every day. What should you shoot first? And what last? Finessing your schedule is something that will probably go on up until the day you start shooting (and beyond), but here's a few things to be aware of:

It's generally a good idea to start in a location where you have a lot of scenes. If, for instance, you have four days scheduled for one character's home, start there. This will give the crew the chance to get into a groove together, and to set a rhythm before hopping around to different locations.

Within those four days, for the sake of actors' performances, it's generally a good idea to stay much in the timeline of the movie (i.e., shooting sequentially as much as possible).

Creating a solid schedule sometimes feels like a Tetris-style puzzle. At this point you don't need it to be perfect. The details will get filled in when you are in pre-production. What matters now is that the overall length of it makes sense, and that you feel confident in your ability to make a great movie in the time you are allowing.

What does a $150,000 budget look like?

I would love to share a budget here that you could use for all your movies, and the work would be done! Unfortunately, it can't work like that, because each and every budget is totally unique to the film that is being made. There is no "boilerplate budget" because there is no "boilerplate film." Where money needs to be spent to make a kickass film will be totally different for each and every movie made.

You might decide that shooting in the desert for five days is essential to your movie (I've made that decision twice). Sure, on one hand it's crazy, because you're going to spend a large percentage of your budget on food and accommodation for your cast and crew, not to mention gas and transport. But on the other hand, if you know that shooting in the desert is what is going to make your movie sing, then you do it, and you keep the reins tight in other areas.

If your film is about a couple of unbelievably fabulous drag queens, you're going to have to put a large chunk of your money into hair, make-up, and wardrobe, but if it's about a middle-aged schoolteacher in Nebraska, you can probably put next to nothing in those departments and max out elsewhere.

All that being said, I'm going to share the top sheet of a budget to give you a general idea of where the money goes, then I'll follow it with some explanations, from my point of view (i.e., a director, not a producer!). Spoiler alert: $150,000 doesn't give you much wiggle room!

Sample Budget

ACCT#	CATEGORY DESCRIPTION	TOTAL
1100	SCRIPT	5,000
1200	PRODUCING	5,000
1300	DIRECTING	5,000
1400	CAST	8,900
	TOTAL ABOVE THE LINE	**23,900**

ACCT#	CATEGORY DESCRIPTION	TOTAL
2100	PRODUCTION STAFF	10,000
2300	ART DIRECTION	5,250
2500	SET DECORATION	6,800
2600	PROPERTY DEPARTMENT	3,700
2700	CAMERA DEPARTMENT	17,500
2800	ELECTRIC DEPARTMENT	9,380
2900	SET OPERATIONS	5,500
3000	PRODUCTION SOUND	4,800
3100	MAKEUP & HAIR DEPARTMENT	2,800
3200	WARDROBE DEPARTMENT	5,250
3600	CATERING & CRAFT SERVICES	7,100
3700	LOCATION DEPARTMENT	8,000
3800	TRANSPORTATION DEPARTMENT	4,500
4800	BTL TRAVEL & LIVING	5,000
	TOTAL PRODUCTION	**95,580**
5100	EDITING	7,500
5200	POST-PRODUCTION FILM & LAB	5,000
5300	POST-PRODUCTION SOUND	10,000
5400	MUSIC	5,000
	TOTAL POST PRODUCTION	**27,500**
6400	GENERAL EXPENSE	1,500
	TOTAL OTHER	**1,500**
9010	CONTINGENCY: 2%	3,020
	Total Above-the-Line	23,900
	Total Below-the-Line	123,080
	Total Above and Below-the-Line	146,980
	GRAND TOTAL	**150,000**

SCRIPT. Very often in microbudget films, the writer gets nothing or next to nothing. That's not right, and I urge you not to accept it. You deserve to be paid, just like everyone else. On big budget films, the writer gets 2.5-5% of the total budget, and that's what the writer deserves.

PRODUCING. I like to keep the three key players (writer, director, producer) on the same level because they each do masses of work for very little, and they work together for a long time. So a sense of equality, and the camaraderie that goes along with that, is important.

DIRECTING. Should directors and producers get paid more than $5,000 given that they will work on the film for a year of their lives? Of course! Sadly, with a budget of $150,000 it's really hard to do that if you want the money to be on the screen (and trust me, you do!). The way to make this sweeter is by writing into their contracts an additional deferred payment, which they will receive when the movie starts to make money. You can write this in so that it is the first money paid out (i.e., before investors get their money back). I wouldn't go crazy with that, but you could add an additional $5,000 to each of them.

CAST. At the time this budget was written, the SAG (actor's union) agreement for ultra low budget films (budgets under $250k) is $125 per day. If you have a lot of speaking parts, you'll notice those fees add up quickly!

So consider cutting back on individual speaking parts. Example: If you have a party scene and you currently have five different people speak in it, could you cut it to three? You'll save $250 right there (and make casting easier).

PRODUCTION STAFF. This includes the super important First Assistant Director (First A.D., who will basically run your set, make sure everyone stays safe, and keep you on schedule), Second Assistant Director (Second A.D.), and Production Assistants (also known as P.A.s). In this case, the First is budgeted at $750/week, Second at $500/week and P.A.s at $75/day. Yes, you could probably get P.A.s for free, but remember what I said before about paying everyone? I meant it. At $75/day they're already earning less than minimum wage, but it will pay their gas money and incentivize them to show up. And dare I say it? They will work so hard, they are worth double that amount.

ART DIRECTION. This covers the fee of the Production Designer: $150/ day for the entire shoot, plus three weeks of prep. You could also negotiate a flat fee.

SET DECORATION. This covers the fee for the Set Decorator, (i.e., an assistant to the Production Designer who's going to help make their vision a reality by building, painting, moving furniture, etc.) as well as the actual budget for paying for the set decoration (which might include paint, purchase or rental of furniture, wall art, etc.).

PROPERTY DEPARTMENT. This includes the fee for the Property Master, as well as money for purchase/rental of props. What is the difference between set material and props? Sometimes it's a fine line, but the Production Designer and Prop Master will figure it out.

CAMERA DEPARTMENT. This is always a big one, as it includes fees for the Director of Photography (also known as the DP), which should probably be around $1500/week for a good one, 1st Camera Assistant, 2nd Camera Assistant, Data Wrangler, and Camera Package Rental. I recommend looking for a DP who has a camera they can rent to you for cheap, or who has strong connections with a rental house, so you can get a great price. That being said, owning great equipment doesn't necessarily make for a great cinematographer, and If I had to choose between a fantastic DP with no equipment and a so-so one with a free Alexa, I'd take the former every time and raise the extra money for the camera hire. For the camera hire, shop around and bargain hard.

ELECTRIC DEPARTMENT. Gaffer, Best Boy and the Electric Package. I'd be looking to pay the crewmembers $150/day, and make that across the board.

SET OPERATIONS. Key Grip and the Grip Package combined costs.

PRODUCTION SOUND. On this kind of budget, I'd seek a one-man (or woman!) band (i.e., someone who can mix and operate the boom simultaneously). It's also a huge bonus if they have their own equipment.

MAKEUP & HAIR DEPARTMENT. Unless you have ambitious plans on the hair and makeup front, I'd try to find a person who can do both. If you have particular days when you're worried they'll be stretched (i.e., you have a party scene with a lot of ladies in it who are going to require attention), bring in extra help just for that day.

WARDROBE DEPARTMENT. Find someone who is *amazing* at thrift store shopping and handy with a sewing machine, and you can keep the budget down. My first film, the total cost of wardrobe was $500! It is possible if you find someone with the right attitude.

CATERING AND CRAFT SERVICE. On our last film, we budgeted $50/day for craft service, and $20/person/day for breakfast and lunch. This is always a tough one for low budget films, because decent, healthy food is essential in so many ways, morale not being the least. Crews love to complain, and shitty food will set them off. Don't let it happen! If you are shooting in a city area, consider "walk away lunches," where you give them each $10 and they go and get their own lunch. Crews love it if there are decent options nearby. If you are using a caterer, take your time to find a really good fit. Good food will make a huge difference to everyone's attitude. Also, don't forget to budget for water. Consider buying each crew member a hydro flask and providing water stations rather than small, disposable plastic bottles. On my last film, shooting in the desert during summer, we not only saved money by doing this, but we also kept a thousand plastic bottles out of the landfill. Win/win!

LOCATION DEPARTMENT. This includes the fees you will pay to rent locations, acquire permits, and hire the equipment you will need to make certain locations work, such as porta-potties, work lights, and dumpsters. Locations can be very expensive, particularly in cities that have a lot of filmmaking going on like LA or NYC. If you *really* want to secure a special location, I recommend creating a relationship with the owner/manager and explaining to them why it's essential for your film. Make it clear that while you don't have a lot of money, you do have a lot of heart! With my first film, I really wanted to shoot in the Museum of Jurassic Technology in Los Angeles. If you haven't been there, it's incredible and just as weird and unique as its name suggests (It's Werner Herzog's favorite place in LA, and David Bowie was a huge fan. Enough said.). No one had filmed there before, despite numerous attempts and big money offers from studios. I pursued it with single-minded dedication. I eventually got to meet with Robert Wilson, the creator of the Museum, and convinced him that the location was an integral part of the story, not just "a cool place to shoot." He read the script, and then let us have the museum for a day—for free!

You will have to pay for some locations, so don't under budget here, because later you may find that you can't make it work. Be realistic. As for permits, be aware of the law in your city/state, and which permits/payments are required. Then make a plan. If you're not going to pay for permits, have a strategy for how you will handle the shoot. I've shot cycling scenes in the streets of LA before without permits (which would have cost a fortune). Our strategy? First, immaculate planning—I knew exactly which streets I wanted to go down and what time the light would be just right, so that on the day of shooting we could get the shots fast without messing around. Second, I took only a skeleton crew out with me, leaving most of the crew at our main location for the day. Smaller groups move faster and are less noticeable. Third, had we been stopped or questioned, I was ready to claim that we were working on a student short video. This is generally a good tactic, even if it's not the truth. Play it down, play naïve, and keep your fingers crossed. Just to be clear: I'm not recommending that you break the law! But the reality of micro budget filmmaking is that sometimes you have to go guerrilla to make it happen. Just be smart about it.

TRANSPORTATION DEPARTMENT. I don't know why, but it kills me that you always have to spend so much of your money on trucks. You need trucks to store and move the equipment, and there's no way around it.

BTL TRAVEL & LIVING. You'll only have to budget for this if you are planning to shoot somewhere away from home base. Any time you take your crew away from home for the night to shoot, you have to put them up in a (semi-) decent hotel, and give them a per diem for each day to cover their basic expenses. It adds up fast! But if you *know* you need that desert location (or mountain, or beach, or whatever), it can be worth it. Breathtaking locations are pure money on the screen, and if you look at it that way it doesn't seem so crazy.

EDITING. Try to negotiate a flat fee with your editor, rather than a weekly rate. This will incentivize her to work diligently, and it will also keep a cap on it.

POST-PRODUCTION FILM & LAB. No one in post works for free, and it's a part of production that you don't want to do super cheap if you want your film to look professional. This fee will cover color correction and deliverables.

POST-PRODUCTION SOUND. Again, negotiate an inclusive deal for a sound package. A good sound mix isn't cheap, but it's worth every penny.

MUSIC. Depending on your film and your aesthetics, you might want to license songs. Be aware that this can be *very* expensive (unless they are an unsigned band and your best mates); so if you want to go down that route, budget accordingly. Otherwise, hire a composer and offer them a single sum ($5,000 for an entire score in this budget gives parity with other key heads of department).

GENERAL EXPENSE. This will cover your insurance—and believe me, you need insurance. Has there ever been a microbudget production that hasn't needed it? If you know of one, I'll eat my shoe.

And there you go: $150,000. It's amazing how fast it all adds up.

Take your time with your budget to get it right. Make sure you are allocating the small amount of money you have to the places that will make your film amazing! Don't spend a penny on anything that feels unnecessary or inessential to your story. Keep asking yourself: What do I really need? What is the essence of the story, and how do I make sure that it shines through? That is all that matters; that your money is being spent in a way that will allow you to make the best film possible.

STEP 4 CHECKLIST

- ☐ Make a list of comparable films and research how much money they made.

- ☐ Decide how much money you'd like for the budget.

- ☐ Let your line producer do their magic.

- ☐ Get real about your script, and make changes to it so that it is doable with the money you aim to raise.

- ☐ Hone the budget and schedule with your line producer until you feel 100% confident that they are doable and realistic.

- ☐ Be grateful for the journey you are on, and celebrate having a realistic plan for how to make your film.

STEP 5
WRITE A
BUSINESS
PLAN

"A goal without a plan is
just a wish."

ANTOINE DE SAINT-EXUPERY
French writer, poet and aviator

YOU HAVE A script, budget, schedule, and start date.

You are beginning to have a clear vision, in your own head, of the film you are making, how you are going to make it and how you are going to sell it. It's time to pull all that information together into a business plan.

I know lots of people panic when they hear those words, but don't freak out! This does not need to be an epic project. It certainly shouldn't take as long as writing your script, and you don't need to hire anyone to do it for you.

It might take the form of an old-fashioned paper essay, or you might want to make it into a power point display. That's your choice, and partly you should make that decision based upon the overall aesthetic and feeling of your film. It is important to organize the overall plan for your movie into a single document that you can easily share with others. Someone else should be able to read the plan and walk away with a clear idea of the film you want to make, how much it will cost, and how you will make the money back. For investors, it might also share what you are offering them (i.e., how the profits of the film will eventually be shared).

Writing a business plan isn't just essential for convincing investors to finance your movie, it's also essential for you. It's your chance to spell out clearly how you imagine this journey might go. It provides you with a road map of your own, and gives you clarity on exactly what your dream is and how you will realize it.

So what do you **need** to cover in your business plan? These are the things that you really can't skip:

WHAT YOUR FILM IS. Start with a log line, followed by a brief synopsis of the film (no more than a page).

WHO IS MAKING IT. Provide brief bios of everyone you know is involved so far. If that's only you, provide your bio. Don't worry if you don't have much film experience so far; be honest, be passionate, be yourself.

WHY IT'S IMPORTANT. This is the director's statement that summarizes the aims of the film artistically, and explains why it's going to be such an awesome, unique movie (even as it might refer to other movies that are like it).

HOW YOU'RE GOING TO MAKE IT. The minimum you need here is the budget top sheet that shows how much you are seeking and how it will be spent.

You may also want to add a section on how you plan to sell the film and split the profits. If you do this, please be aware that by law, you must also clearly lay out the risks involved in investing in films. It's like how drug companies must state the possible negative side effects of the wonder pill they're touting. In this case, you must clearly state that developing, producing and distributing movies is a high-risk investment, and that in most cases the money is lost.

I know it's a downer, and we all want to be super positive all of the time, but it's just not cool to present a case to investors that is based on pipe dreams. Be honest—and please don't quote the crazy profits of movies like *The Blair Witch Project* or *My Big Fat Greek Wedding* in your business plan. Sure, there is a tiny chance that your film will be that one-in-ten-million, knockout hit, but statistically the odds are not in your favor. Impress potential investors instead with your diligence and truthfulness, and show them how you're in touch with the real world. That is far more likely to engage their trust in you, and consequently, their financial support.

So, what would you be offering your investors in the business plan? A typical payout structure for an indie film: The financial investors will receive 120% of their investment back, after which profits will be split 50/50 with the filmmakers. Now note I said "typical." There's no law on this and you can offer what you want. So perhaps, acknowledging the high-risk nature of their investment, you want to offer them a 25% return before profits are split with you. Go for it. Or maybe you want to pay out deferred salaries before investors receive their money back? You can do that too, and explain why (i.e., that your director is investing their time and skills for below market rate, a.k.a. "sweat equity").

As you work on this, clarify what you think is a fair model for your film. Create one in which both financial investors, as well as key cast and crew, will be justly rewarded if the film is a hit.

Remember though, you should not spend months writing a business plan. In fact, if you've got all your backup materials (i.e., you've got the budget and script on hand), it really shouldn't take more than a day or two—and then perhaps a day to format it to make it look great.

Is there a formula for how it should look? Absolutely not.

Creating a film is like creating a world, and ideally everything connected to it (both before and after production) should feel like a part of that world, so be creative with the look of your business plan. Take the time to find the fonts that invoke the feeling of your movie. Perhaps change the color of the pages and the letters. Don't be afraid to use photos; you're going to get some perfect ones when you shoot a concept video (Step 7).

At this point, your business plan will be a work in progress, as you won't actually finish it and share it until you have completed the next couple of steps, but it's important to get started on it now, as later you will be busy with a lot of other tasks!

In total, you should aim for your business plan to be no more than five pages. People are busy—respect that, and keep it succinct. Make it snappy, clear, and full of energy and buzz. Fill it with the passion and excitement you honestly feel when you think about your film, and don't be afraid to give it unique character. A good film business plan is infused with the spirit of your movie—and for the right person, that will be irresistible.

STEP 5 CHECKLIST

- ☐ Gather all the information you need for your business plan.
- ☐ Write it out.
- ☐ Add pictures, play with the fonts, and make it look like how your film feels.
- ☐ Be grateful for the journey you are on, and celebrate how clear and concise your business plan is.

STEP 6
FIND KEY
CREW AND
CAST

"Filmmaking is all about
appreciating the talents
of the people you
surround yourself with
and knowing you could
never have made any of
these films by yourself."

STEVEN SPIELBERG
master storyteller and director of
Jaws, E.T. and *Schindler's List*

YOU'VE GOT A road map for making your movie; you know how much money you need, and how to spend that money to make a great movie . . . but you still need to get those dollars in the bank.

The next two steps are directly related to making the secret sauce that makes financing easy. Yes, you read that right: *easy*.

They are also incredibly smart steps to take to ensure that ultimately you make the best film you possibly can. These two steps are win/win—don't skip them or plan to do them later (i.e., after trying to raise finance) if you're serious about making a truly standout film.

Right now, before you have approached investors, is the time to find some of your key creative collaborators, namely your Director of Photography, editor, and key cast. You're also going to find a Producer of Marketing and Distribution.

You're going to need them now, partly so that you can add their names and bios to your business plan, but also so that you can shoot a terrific, enticing concept trailer.

Director of Photography

This is one of the most important collaborators that you will work with in making your movie.

Look at the name of the job: *Director* of Photography.

Their job is the look of your film. In one sense, you are the director of actors, and they are looking after the camera.

So many films fail, or are just plain mediocre, because the DP isn't that great. Film is a visual medium, so it's essential that the images are top quality.

A great DP will elevate your material. They will have a great sense of composition, and of color. They will be inspired by the same visual artists and references that you are, and they will inspire you. They will take your vision and double it. They will make everything look even better than it did in your head.

Please then: Do not go with someone just because they have the gear. Gear is easy to get; a great eye isn't.

Do not shoot your film yourself *unless* you would be hired by someone else to be their Director of Photography. Truly. Don't even think about it. Sure, I know what many of you are thinking: You have a Canon HD and you're pretty handy with it. Why not slash the budget and DIY it?

Trust me: If you want to make a *standout* indie, unless you are exceptionally good behind a camera, don't even think about it. Be honest about your talents and your goals. Do you want to be a Director of Photography? Is that part of your dream? Are you working towards that diligently every day? If it is, then cool. Shoot your movie. But if it's not, take the time to find the person who dreams of being the cameraperson.

Ultimately, your film will be as good as all the people who make it, so find the best you can.

Does this mean that you have to find someone with a thousand credits? No. Find someone with a good eye, and trust your instincts.

With my first film, Matt Medlin, our line producer, suggested a friend of his, Zak Mulligan, to shoot the film. Zak had done a lot of shorts and music videos, but had never shot a feature. I talked with Zak on the phone, and immediately we clicked. When I referenced Paris, Texas and the films of Truffaut, he knew what I was talking about. He seemed visually ambitious, and most importantly, he seemed to really love the script. We agreed to shoot some tests together. He paid for his own ticket from NYC to LA, and brought his RED camera.

Within minutes of that test shoot, I knew I'd found my DP. He found the picture that was in my head; but every time, he made it look even better. No, he had never shot a feature before, but I knew in my heart he would do a great job. And he did: He went on to win the prize for best cinematography at Sundance for our film, beating out super-experienced cinematographers with one hundred times our budget.

Again and again I'll say it: Hire the people you love, and who you feel get your vision. Hire the people who show genuine passion for your script, and will go the extra distance to make it with you. If those people are not super experienced, don't sweat it! If the chemistry is right, and the drive is there, you will make magic together. Guaranteed.

So how do you go about finding a great Director of Photography? These strategies are pretty much the same for finding any crew:

- Watch films (both features and shorts) made in your area, and if any cinematography stands out to you, reach out to the DP. DPs are often willing to travel for the right project, so also reach out to people from out of town if you feel passionately that they are the right fit for your film.

- Ask friends who make films if they have any recommendations.

- Go to your local film school and ask about recent graduates and students.

- Put an ad on Craigslist! And if that doesn't work for you, try a social media shout-out (i.e., post that you are looking on your Facebook, Twitter, etc.).

- Go to local filmmaker networking events and local film festivals to meet people.

Finally, here are the qualities that I think are non-negotiable when it comes to choosing your Director of Photography. If they satisfy all of these, you've found a winner!

HIRING A DP

- They have a great eye for composition and color. See their previous work!

- They work fast. Talk to them about their approach, and how they'd handle shooting a lot of great material on a tight schedule.

- They are good team players—trust your gut!

- They are inventive within the constraints of a small budget.

- They think out of the box.

- They share a passion for your visual references.

Editor

You might be thinking, *"Editor? Why the heck would I need an editor now?!"*

The reason is that soon, very soon, you're going to be shooting a concept trailer, and you're going to need someone to cut it. You'll also be making a crowdfunding campaign video, so you'll need an editor for that, too.

Now, it is possible you are pretty good on Final Cut yourself. If you are, by all means, you can probably get away without adding another person to your crew just yet. However, under no circumstances would I recommend editing your entire feature by yourself, even if you make your living as an editor. When you get to that stage, objective eyes are crucial if you are going to make an excellent film.

It also makes sense to find someone now, so you can start building a relationship and a creative understanding with them. Cutting the concept trailer will give you a sense if this is your ideal collaborator.

The relationship you will have with your editor is so specific. You will literally spend months together in a dark room, just the two of you. So it better be someone you enjoy spending time with, or you're both going to go crazy!

Besides being an awesome person who laughs at your jokes, it really helps if they have a strong sense of story, an impeccable sense of rhythm and an objective disposition. You'll be able to tell this when you work on the concept trailer with them. Do they just follow your instructions, or do they add value, contributing genius ideas of their own? That's what you want—someone with the right sensibility who also brings fresh eyes and perspective to the material you've shot.

It's no surprise that many great directors (Quentin Tarantino and Martin Scorsese spring immediately to mind) always work with the same editor. Really they're one of the most essential collaborators you'll have in this process, so take your time to find someone you absolutely love.

Producer of Marketing and Distribution

A PMD is a fairly new concept, but a truly worthy one. You have your producers who are engaged in raising money, hiring crew, pulling together your production, but often, particularly with microbudgeted movies, by the time you get to post production or to your festival run, they're busy with new shoots and other projects. They have to pay their rent like everyone, and typically, the money from your film ran out a long time ago. This is when a producer whose sole responsibility will be marketing and handling the distribution of your film takes the reins.

Of course, you could wait until after you have shot your concept trailer to engage this individual, but it's smart to do it now, as the earlier that they are involved, the better.

The ideal PMD will be visionary, ambitious, and super savvy on social media. This is such a new role that you may not be able to find someone who has done it before. Rather, you might find someone with the experience of seeing films through distribution or film marketing. Ultimately, they will plan, create a distribution budget, and then hire a team to execute it.

We'll talk a lot more about all this later . . . but for now, just be aware that the sooner you have this person involved, the smarter your choices will be over the next few steps.

Key Cast

CONVENTIONAL WISDOM: Attach the biggest names you can. Check their IMDb starmeter rating, check out how many followers they have on Twitter, check their credits.

REBEL HEART WAY: Cast the people who are best for the roles and who are the most committed.

I'll repeat that: They should be right for the role and also committed.

The rest is noise.

Think about some of the biggest standout indie films from the last few years: *Beasts of the Southern Wild*?! Do you think it would have been half as good had they cast Willow Smith in the lead role? No! They cast a complete unknown . . . and she was nominated for an Oscar.

Think about it.

Be bold, be brave, and go with your heart. Find someone who you just flat out *love* for the part. Someone who is fantastic in the role and excites you beyond belief. Someone who will go to the end of the world for you. That is the collaborator you want and need.

You might still be thinking: *But everyone says cast is key. If you have names, you'll get distribution. You need names to sell a film. It's common sense.*

And you know, you're absolutely right. If you're budgeting your film over $500,000 you really should get name talent. It's a lot harder to recoup $500,000 than $100,000, and you will most likely need a foreign sales component to make your money back.

If you are going down the name route, be really smart about it. Only some names are really meaningful when it comes to distribution. The fact that actor A had a small part in a big movie doesn't mean anything to potential audiences, or distributors, so don't be dazzled by a couple of fancy credits on an actor's resume.

First and foremost, cast them because you think they'll be *amazing* in your part. If you're only going after them because they have a million Instagram followers, forget it. They have to be right for the role or there's no point.

Second, make sure that their brand fits the brand of your film. If that sounds horrifically businesslike, forgive me. But seriously, ask yourself the following questions of any actor: What do they represent? Who loves them and would go see anything they did? Are they the same as the people who would love your movie?

Typically, you'll find it's very hard to get a very big name to do a small movie, unless they get to play against type. Think about it: if a young starlet is always cast as a sex symbol and gets paid lots of money for it, why is she going to play that same part in your movie for peanuts? However, if you give her the chance to play a brainy scientist, she might do it, because it gives her the chance to show she can do something different. The problem for you, when it comes to marketing the film, is whether an audience will want to see her in this kind of role. That depends on whether she has the acting chops to pull it off. So, if you are going to go down this route, make sure the actor, as stated before, really is *right* for the role.

I know many people in LA who have been trying to attach name talent to their movies for years. Literally years, and they are still no closer to making their movies. It pays to be realistic. If you are a first-time filmmaker with very little money, and you don't have a known producer or big shot casting agent, it is highly unlikely that you are going to snag an A-lister for your film. I'm not going to say impossible, because nothing is, but if you just want to make your damn movie already, forget the fancy names, and find the untapped talent.

One caveat: If you are obsessed with the idea of a certain actor playing a part in your film, by all means give it a serious shot to get the script to them. The very first screenplay I wrote was called *Mickey and Me*. It was about Mickey Rourke and the Mexican voice-over actor who dubbed all his movies into Spanish. It was set in the time when Mickey's career was in the doldrums, and the movie was about this Mexican voice-over actor coming to LA to find Mickey and get him back on top.

When I wrote it, I was living in Barcelona, Spain, but I knew a few people in the British film industry, so I sent the script to them. They all came back with "it's a nice writing sample, but you'll never get it made, because you'll never get Mickey." I set in my mind that, until Mickey himself said no, I wasn't going to take no for an answer. So when I learned that he was going to be at the Cannes Film Festival (with *Sin City* in 2005), I hired a car, and drove there with copies of my script in hand.

Despite my valiant attempts, I didn't meet Mickey at Cannes—but I did meet a producer who, a month later, told another LA producer, Peter Samuelson, about my script. At that time, Peter was making a movie with none other than Mickey Rourke. He emailed me and asked to see the script. He read it, loved it and asked if he could show it to Mickey. Six months after the Cannes film festival, I was sitting at a café in Los Angeles taking notes from Mickey Rourke on changes he wanted made to my script.

Sadly, the movie never did get made, but it did kickstart my screenwriting career . . . and it taught me the importance of having a vision and being insanely tenacious. Had I listened to those British producers, I would have given up before I even started. If you are 100% certain that some actor is *the* one for your film, it's your job to get it to them. Just because one person says it's not possible, doesn't mean you should give up. Obviously I'm not advocating that you should become an obsessed stalker, but you owe it to yourself to pursue your dream with all your heart. If you're not that passionate about it, who will be?!

Back to the issue of casting unknown actors in your film. I originally developed the lead character in my first movie for an actor I knew; let's call him Joe. Joe works all the time. He isn't a star, but he's a solid working character actor with a string of decent credits to his name—indies, big studio films as well as TV shows.

Joe seemed super excited about getting the chance to play the lead in my film, and was really keen for the female lead to be equal in stature to him, if not even more of a "star." To that end, Joe shared the script with an actress he worked with, the star of a network TV show, who at the time was in the top hundred on the IMDb "star meter." She loved the script and wanted to do it.

Her manager loved it too. He saw it as a chance for her to be seen in something other than her TV character. He wanted us to raise the budget from $140k to over $500k and said he could get the money. In my heart though, I wanted Gaynor Howe to play the female lead. Gaynor is a very old friend of mine from my university days in Scotland, who had worked as an actress, but never got the breaks and had largely given up on it. I knew that she was perfect for the role.

Once I knew that Zak was coming to LA for the camera test, I asked Gaynor to come over from London (where she lives) to be a part of it. I was certain that once Joe met her and had the chance to work with her, he'd give up on the idea of the network star as his leading lady, and that he would be as excited as I was about Gaynor.

So, Zak flew in from NY with the camera, and Gaynor flew in from London (both on their own dime). I set up the test shoot: a weekend out in Death Valley. Motel rooms were booked, tents were packed, food and water bought for the crew . . . and then the night before we left for the desert, Joe phoned me. He couldn't come. He had an audition for a pilot on Monday, and said he needed the weekend to prepare for it.

It was devastating. It was 10:00 pm on Friday night, and we were meant to leave at 6:00 AM the next morning to go to the desert—but now we didn't have a lead actor.

My husband Chris had the idea to call an actor he had met recently, Michael Piccirilli ("Pitch"). I was initially reticent; he was far too good-looking, nothing like the character of George. But given the situation, I decided it was worth calling him. We were desperate. A hungry actor who was up for adventure, Pitch agreed to come with us the next morning.

Off we went to the desert the next day, and it was there that the craziest thing happened. Pitch put on the glasses I had bought for the character of George, and there he was. George. Unquestionably.

Furthermore, the chemistry between Pitch and Gaynor was perfect. I couldn't have hoped for better. The key roles were cast.

Joe was very upset when I let him know he'd lost the role, but it had become clear to me was that he wasn't committed. If a better offer had come up, he would have jumped ship in a heartbeat.

The single most important thing that will make your movie soar is this: Everyone working on it loves it like it is theirs, and puts their own heart and soul into it.

They will come to the desert and give it their all. They will have your back every step of the way, just as you will have theirs. They will go the extra mile, and the mile beyond that, without question.

This dedication and love is what will give your movie the

edge over every other film out there. That is how your film will end up being more than the sum of its parts.

And it starts with the casting.

So, how do I go about finding actors?

There are so many ways.

You can cast your friends. Find people from other films, or from your local theater.

Talk with anyone who engages and excites you.

And then put them in front of a camera, and see if they work.

This is essential. I wouldn't cast anyone without seeing them on film. It's a strange fact that some people look quite dull in life, but come alive on camera. Others have the opposite problem (in the room, they are amazing, but on film, just boring). I don't know what that quality is, but it's really true that the camera loves some people (and other people, it just goes "meh").

If you get them to read lines, look for their ability to handle **subtext.** To me, the biggest difference between good and great acting is the ability to convey feelings without speaking, and the ability to say one thing and mean something else. Bad actors tend to be very literal. They lack nuance, and it's nuance that engages us.

All the great actors have a sense of an inner life. You can't help watching them. You want to know what they are going to do next. If you try your friend on camera, and you get that feeling, go for it, whether they have a million followers or not. You have found your perfect star.

STEP 6 CHECKLIST

- ☐ Research your options for DP, editor, PMD and actors.
- ☐ Meet with anyone who you think might be right.
- ☐ Trust your gut, and go with the people you love.
- ☐ Be grateful for the journey you are on, and celebrate by inviting your growing team to a dinner at your house. You are going to have the time of your lives together.

STEP 7
SHOOT A
CONCEPT
TRAILER

"If you don't know where
you are going, you'll end
up someplace else."

YOGI BERRA
legendary baseball catcher

IT'S STARTING TO come together. You have a team, and you have a solid plan.

It's time to shoot a concept trailer!

Why? What's the point?

This is going to be absolutely crucial for raising finance; there is nothing more persuasive to a potential investor than seeing footage that makes them want to see the movie.

You're going to test drive your DP, your actors, and the overall look of your film. This will put you in a much stronger position for success on your actual shoot.

So, what is a concept trailer?

Let's start with what is not: It is not a "sizzle reel" (how I hate that term!). It's not a collection of clips from other movies that you think are comparable to your movie. I don't know what that shows to anyone, besides the fact that you know some cool movies.

It is like a trailer for a completed film.

It will introduce the main characters, as well as the setting, tone and mood of your film.

It will show a possible financier that this movie is going to look amazing and totally professional, and it will give them a real sense of what to expect.

It shouldn't be longer than a couple of minutes (Like a trailer, leave them wanting more!).

So, how do I make an effective one?

To take away the mystery, I have created a simple formula that is cheap, straightforward, and gives you the chance to make something terrific in a very short amount of time. Here it is:

1. **You will shoot for two days, perhaps only one** – Yay! This is how you keep it cheap—one-day camera rental!

2. **You will shoot MOS (which stands for** *"motor only shot"*—**i.e., you will not record sound)** – This is how you keep it fast, and allow yourself to shoot lots of footage. Not worrying about sound means you can grab shots in many different locations without worrying about the noise. It also means the actors can improvise—getting lines right doesn't matter.

3. **You will collect images and moments that show a broad range of scenarios in the film** – This will make your final trailer look like the trailer for a completed film. It's not just one location or one scene. It shows a whole bunch of different scenarios.

4. **You will make sure that some of these moments display the central conflicts (or dramas) of your story** – This is crucial. Miss this, and you end up with pretty pictures, leaving the jaded viewer to ask, "so what?!" Think about the main conflicts in your movie. What is the hook of your film? What are the emotional high points? Be sure you include some of those, otherwise it will be a big yawn.

5. **On a different day, after the shoot, you will record a voice-over from the POV of one of your characters –** This could be based on a monologue they deliver in the script, or it could be totally written for this purpose only. You could also make it from the perspectives of two (or more) of the characters in your film.

6. **You will now edit the images to a piece of music and your voiceover . . .**

and voila!

You have a concept trailer.

This formula works whether your film is a melancholy drama, a comedy or a horror. This formula works. Period. If you use it, I promise it will set you on the road to getting your film made like nothing else. You will also get a clearer view of the film you are trying to make. It's like doing a sketch before a painting—your painting will be so much better for it. Trust me.

Here are some FAQs about making a concept trailer:

How do I choose which scenes to shoot?

Go through your script, and highlight the strongest scenes emotionally. Once you have two of these (that hopefully take place in different locations), think about finding two more scenes that have different emotional currents.

Think about the music and the voice-over. What is the story that you are trying to tell in the trailer? What moments in your film would help show that?

Start a list of the scenes or moments you'd like to capture. I usually have an idea of the ones I must get and the ones I'd like to get if I have time. Prioritize your shooting schedule accordingly.

How much should I try to shoot?

Really as much as you can without losing quality of the images. Remember, you want this to look awesome. This will be your calling card, so you don't want crappy lighting, bad compositions, etc. You want every image to sell your film as a professional, brilliant movie.

Since you're not trying to get sound, you should be able to move fast, so aim high, and plan to work your butt off on the day.

What crew will I need?

The non-negotiables, who you will need no matter what: your cast, a cinematographer, one assistant.

Then it depends what you're trying to achieve. If you need special hair and make-up, you'll need someone for that. If you require detailed costuming, plan on having a wardrobe person. If you're going to shoot a lot of interiors and want specific lighting, you might need to enlist a gaffer.

A word of advice? Keep it as slim as possible. If you don't *need* a wardrobe person, don't have one. Often the more crew you have, the slower things can get.

How much will it cost?

As you already know, I'm pretty obsessed with cast and crew

being paid for their work, however this is the one time that I ask people to work for free. After all, this is their chance to pitch for a paid gig (your feature film), just as it is yours.

If you get them to work for free though, you'd better make it fun and treat them really well. Make sure you factor in decent food for them, and the price of a few bottles of beer or wine for when you've wrapped.

Even if your cast and crew will work for free, there are still some unavoidable costs:

- Camera and equipment rental
- Food for cast and crew (make it good and keep them happy!)
- Accommodation costs (if you go out of town)
- Hard drives for storing data
- Some costume, set decoration, props
- Insurance

In my experience, it's possible to do all of this for around $2,000 and still make it look incredible (and it has to look incredible, there's no reason to do it otherwise).
Where do I get the money?

This is one and only time where I suggest putting down your credit card or using your own savings. You will have it in your budget as development costs, so once you raise finance for the film, you will get this money back. See it as an investment in your own dream.

Obviously, there is a risk involved. You might not raise the money for your film, and in that case, you'll end up out of pocket (but if you're thinking like that at this stage, you might as well quit and go home now). I think it's a risk worth taking, but take it only if it's realistic for you. If you need to borrow the money (i.e., on a credit card or from your folks), obviously you should only borrow as much as you are confident that you can repay fairly easily. Don't put yourself into a situation of stress. It's not worth it.

If $2,000 is definitely beyond your reach, what is within your reach? What is the dollar amount that you can raise to make this happen? Write down that sum and figure out a budget for that amount. Find a way to make it work. That's what indie filmmakers do.

You could consider doing a crowdfunding campaign to raise the money to shoot this, and if you are totally new to filmmaking, that is not a bad idea. You'll begin to gather a tribe for your film very early on, and involve other people, and that can help create momentum for you. We'll discuss crowdfunding in more detail later, but know now: It's a great tool for every indie filmmaker, and if you've never done it before, it might be cool to do it now with a smaller amount as your goal.

The Creative Upside

The reason to shoot a concept trailer isn't just to raise money. It's also to develop your film in a more visual, cinematic way. It's particularly crucial if it's your first film, but always a great thing to do.

When you start the shoot, as you are not trying to get sound, allow yourself to be free, to be open. Be alert to possibilities. Magic happens when you allow it. If you are too busy trying to get what you *think* you need, you might miss the perfect moment. Follow your instincts and have fun! Allow yourself the joy of discovery on this shoot. You don't have any real pressure. You're just trying to gather awesome looking material that will sell your film, that will make people want to see it. Stay focused on that and you'll make something spectacular.

Having the chance to work with actors and your DP in real locations is an incredible luxury. You can explore and test the visual look of the film. You can lay great groundwork with your actors. You can explore ideas for scenes, test them, turn them inside out, and see what works.

Doing a shoot like this? It's win/win/win.

After the shoot

If you haven't done so already, choose some music. If you are only going to use the trailer for raising finance (i.e., you're never going to show it publically), you can use pretty much anything. If you plan on putting it on YouTube and generating a lot of traffic to it, it's better to use something you own the rights to.

If you plan to work with a composer on your feature, this can be a good time to get them involved, and ask them to create something for you.

In any case, the music you choose is going to be such an aesthetically significant part of this that it's important to get it right. Even if it's not something you'll eventually use in your completed film, it should hit the right tone emotionally.

Also, check the length—you definitely don't want anything over three minutes. Attention spans are short, so keep it snappy.

After you have selected the music, record the voice-over with your actor (or actors). Make sure you get them to leave space between each sentence so that you can cut the voice-over, and adapt it in the final edit. Feel free to record more lines than you think you'll need! It's easy to lose lines when you're making the final edit, but a pain if you have to go back and record more.

Now you are ready to cut your trailer with your editor. Make sure you use your best material, and that the trailer has an emotional arc to it. Once you think it's done, show it to a couple of friends and get feedback. Hone it until you LOVE it and desperately want to share it with the world.

You now have something very concrete to share.

Well done, you! You now have the complete package you need, and you're ready to raise finance. Woot!!!

STEP 7 CHECKLIST

- ☐ Choose the moments you want to shoot.
- ☐ Plan your shoot: locations and camera hire.
- ☐ Have a blast shooting some scenes.
- ☐ Edit it, add music and a voice-over.
- ☐ Be grateful for the journey you are on, and celebrate by hosting a party and sharing your awesome trailer with your collaborators.

STEP 8
START AN
LLC, RAISE
THE MONEY

"Every day's a hustle."

RICHARD LINKLATER
writer/director of *Slacker, School of Rock, Before Sunrise* and *Boyhood*

BEFORE YOU START to raise money, you should set up an LLC so that when you get a financier on the hook, you are ready to accept a check from them before they have the chance to change their mind!

The laws are different in each state, so go online and check what the rules are where you live. In some places it's super cheap and easy to do, but in others it isn't. You may be able to do it yourself, although I recommend you consult with a lawyer to set up your LLC and operating agreement.

For movies, your typical LLC is a single purpose entity (i.e., the purpose of the company is to make X movie and to exploit it). You will set up a separate LLC for each film you make (even if you have a production company that is making more than one). This is so that money invested in the movie is for that movie only.

It does cost some cash to set up an LLC, but there are many reasons to do it—mostly concerned with protecting you from liability, as well as making you legitimate in the eyes of an investor. If money is very tight, you can wait to set it up until after you have some finance in place.

Now, time for the million-dollar question, the one that indie filmmakers sweat about more than any other:

Where do I find the money?

The very first thing I am going to say about this: stop sweating.

As long as you think that *the thing* that is stopping you from being a fabulously successful filmmaker is that you don't have any money, it will continue to be a problem. Forever.

So here's the deal: The money is out there.

You just need to find it.

And to find it, you have to make an enticing, exciting proposition; you have to be offering a package that people naturally want to be a part of.

Which is exactly why you've been working your butt off for the past seven steps, creating a package that no sane person would say no to.

So if you've done the groundwork, you can relax. You will get the money.

When it comes to raising finance, here are two bulletproof rules for success:

RULE #1: Do not be desperate. Seriously. If you feel like you have to beg people, you are missing the point. People will not give you money if they sense that energy around you.

RULE #2: The more confident you are, the more people will have confidence in you. Would you hand someone a check for $100,000 if they can't make eye contact, and are shaking as they talk to you? Of course not!

Investors want to feel confident that you know what you are doing. That their money is safe with you. That you are the captain of a ship they feel excited to board.

It's that simple.

So where will you actually get it? Who do you approach?

I'm going to suggest two main sources: private equity and crowdfunding.

Private Equity

This is going to be a major source of your budget, money from individuals who want to invest in your movie. Before you think "but I don't know any billionaires!"— I don't either. You don't need to.

Here's what you are going to do:

1. Make a list of every wealthy person you know. They don't have to be crazy rich, just people you know who have some disposable income. Like your dentist. Or your boss. Or your old school principle (if you were a good student!). Anyone you know who might have $5,000 that they could afford to lose.

2. Make a list of every person who has ever expressed support for you and your creative work. They may be rich, poor, or anything in between.

3. Make another list of anyone you know who has invested in the arts before (not just film). It might be a person you know who buys pottery, or frequently goes to live music concerts.

4. If you went to college, do some research and make a list of alumni who have done well financially. Also, write down the name of your Alumni Association.

5. Make a list of people (or organizations) who might have special interests in your film. For instance, if

your film is about a family dealing with the mother's Alzheimer's, put down "Alzheimer's associations." Time for more research!

If you have zero people on any of these lists, please don't despair! But if you have zero, you're doing it wrong. Go back to the first list (wealthy people). Again, they don't need to be out of this world, lottery winner rich. Just people who aren't struggling for cash. The owner of a local restaurant that you frequent, for example.

Now look at these lists.

You will leave no stone unturned. You are going to raise finance from these people.

First, look to see if anyone's name shows up on more than one list. If you know someone who has cash to spare, supports your work always, and has invested in the arts before, think of that person as a slam-dunk. They will almost certainly invest in your film.

Next, consider those that you think could invest larger amounts, as generally you will work from larger to smaller.

It's worth noting that for some people it's ideal to get just one or two financiers, and the fewer the better, but I'm not sure about this. If you have a single investor, they will feel like they have ownership of the film, and that could be problematic down the line, whereas if you get money from many sources, no one feels like they have ownership over the film—except for you—and that gives you greater creative freedom. One of my students raised $500,000 for her film by selling $5,000 shares. She made it an exciting experience for her entire community. Obviously some investors bought multiple shares, but you can see the possibilities.

Given that you are also going to raise money from crowdfunding (spoiler alert: that's our next step), the final overall picture might be:

Crowdfunding	$40,000
Investor 1	$40,000
Investor 2	$20,000
Investor 3	$10,000
Investor 4	$10,000
TOTAL:	**$120,000**

Let's also remember that you may not need your entire budget in the bank before you start. Sure, that's the conventional way, but in truth, you really only need enough money to get you through physical production. You could raise the money for post later. So, if your shoot is going to cost $60,000, aim to get at least that much in the bank first. By the time you finish physical production, you'll have awesome footage to show as you go to raise the remaining funds. It's worth noting that this approach is not for the faint of heart. You need courage, and faith that you *will* raise the rest of the money. But I'm going to tell you now: you *can* do this. I know you can, because I've done it, and I'm no one special.

Be bold, and have no fear. If you're totally passionate about your film and you want to make it with all your heart, you will do it. Nothing can stop you. Be single-minded and make "tenacious" your middle name.

The Psychology of Raising Finance

I cannot stress enough how important it is that you are confident about what you are offering. You must simultaneously ooze excitement, seriousness, and passion for your film (that sounds kinda weird, but run with it . . .).

This is why you have done all this groundwork, so that you can meet with anyone and say: *"Here's the script. Here's the budget and schedule. Here's a trailer that shows you how awesome it's going to be. We're starting on this date. This train is leaving the station, are you in?"*

Don't beg. Don't be desperate. Don't undervalue yourself or your project.

Be clear about this with yourself: You are offering your potential investors the opportunity to be involved in something fantastic, magical, meaningful and creative. How many times does that happen in your life?!

People invest money in movies for very different reasons. It might be simply because they believe in you (your Uncle Ted, for instance!). It might be because they feel passionately about the subject matter of your film, and want to help get that message out there. Perhaps it's because they want their son or daughter to be a part of it (and yes, if the deal is they'll contribute $20,000 if their kid gets to be an intern or land a small speaking role, go with it). Or it might be because they themselves are excited about the idea of being part of a movie—they want to come to set, and they look forward to the fun of the film's premier. It's truly not about return on investment for these people, and in my mind, these are the people you want to pursue as investors. People who want to be part of the ride because of the ride ... not because of where they think it's going.

Before you go to meet any potential investor, remind yourself: You don't need that particular investor—there are plenty of other places to get money—but they need you to have this experience! When else will they have the chance to be involved with something as cool, important, fun, awesome, and life-changing as this?

I often start the conversation with a potential investor casually, with a text message rather than email. Something along the lines of *"Hey Bob, I'm planning to shoot a film this summer. So excited about it! We are bringing some more investors on board and I thought of you. I wonder if you'd have time for a chat about it? No pressure at all! Just think it would be great to have you involved; it really is going to be a special experience."*

Keeping it casual is important, because it doesn't make them feel that you need them. They sense that you are not desperate, and that will increase their confidence in you.

The next step, once they agree to chat with you about it, is to make your potential investor feel special: *"I came to you because I really admire you, and I've always wanted to work with you. I feel like this is going to be an amazing experience that I know you will love, and I think it would be incredible for you to be a part of this, etc. ... "*

At the same time, make it clear that the project is coming together beautifully; that it's going to happen regardless of whether they invest or not. People hate missing out. If they feel it's happening and it's going to be brilliant, they will want to be a part of it, guaranteed.

If you do get a "no" from someone you really hoped would pull through for you, take a breath, and consider their reason. Some people are worth pursuing further, even after they have said no, because some people like to be pursued. Strike that. Some people *need* to be pursued. It's your persistence that will convince them your project is worth investing in. If you're not willing to fight for your film, why should someone put their money into it? Of course, don't be an asshole, and know when to back off. But as the saying goes, sometimes "no" is the beginning of a conversation.

Once you have one investor, it usually becomes easier to get more. The first one is definitely the hardest. Again, people like to invest in "sure things," so if you've got 90% of your finance, finding 10% isn't hard, but finding the first 10% can be brutal.

Here's a tried and tested solution to this: lie. Oh boy, I can't believe I just said that either, because I'm generally all about telling the truth, but I stumbled on this method by accident, and it works. When you reach out to an investor, say *"I'm shooting this film, starting Jan 2, and one of our investors just dropped out so we have a shortfall. I thought of you, and wondered if you'd be interested in this opportunity?"*

Okay, so there was no other investor who dropped out . . . but somehow the idea that someone was in, and now they're not, can make it more appealing. I don't think it's a terrible lie because the truth is you need that money! If shaping the presentation makes them more eager to jump in, I say go for it.

However, honesty about what you are offering is everything. Seriously:

Make sure you are always 100% honest about the risks involved in investing in a film. Do not lie. Do not pretend they are going to get rich from it. Do not allow anyone to invest money that they can't afford to lose.

Sometimes a potential investor will ask me: how much do you need? To which I'll say, "We're still short $60,000, but honestly I'd want you to invest only as much as you would be comfortable with losing completely. I'm going to do everything I can to make the money back and a profit, but I value our friendship too much, etc." This kind of honesty wins you trust, and your friend is a thousand times more likely to write a check when they know you are being straight with them. Don't risk your friendship, your reputation and someone else's cash on falsehoods. It's bad karma, and it's distinctly not cool.

The most important quality

To be an indie filmmaker you need to develop a single-minded tenacity.

Nothing can stop you.

People will say no.

You keep coming at them.

You do not give up.

You are a filmmaking zombie, and they can shoot all they like at you.

You keep coming at them.

Don't be an asshole about it, but seriously, if you want to make a movie, you have to develop the ability to push through the "noes."

The money is out there.

Don't sweat it.

Go get it.

There are, of course, other ways to finance your film, such as grants, foreign pre-sales, and money from production companies.

Grants

There are a number of great grants and awards out there that can help you make your film.

For narrative films in the US, these include (but are not limited to):

- Film Independent Fast Track Fellowship
- Creative Capital
- Women in Film/Netflix Finishing Fund
- The Roy Dean Grant/From the Heart Productions
- Netpix/Firstpix Crowdfunding Grant
- San Francisco Film Fund
- Alfred P. Sloan Fellowship
- Cinereach

These are definitely worth exploring, as they say: It takes a village to make a film, and to have the support of one of these organizations is amazing. But I don't want you to see these as the be-all and end-all.

If you think you or your film is a fit for one or more of them, go for it! You have nothing to lose except the time it takes to write your submission/proposal.

But please know that if you don't get money this way, your entrepreneurial spirit can win the day. By focusing on raising private equity, you will make your film whether you get grants or not.

Foreign Pre-sales

You've probably read in the trades about films getting financed by selling foreign rights at Cannes or the American Film Market (AFM).

This path has become more difficult in recent years, but in any case would be totally dependent on cast, director, and genre. If you are packaging a film with recognizable name talents, a known director, and a sellable genre (i.e., horror or thriller), then it's absolutely worth considering. On the other hand, if you're planning to make a comedy or drama with no known names, forget about it. You will be wasting your time.

A subset of this path is to access money from foreign co-productions. Many European film commissions offer serious finance for movies that will either shoot or have post-production in their country. If you think that might be a fit for your film, you will need to get a producer from that country involved in order to be eligible to apply.

Production Companies

And yes, of course you can get finance from a company whose sole business is to make movies.

This is a conventional route to making a movie: Pitch it to companies, and sell it.

One word about this: If it does get picked up, the film will no longer be yours.

On one hand, it's awesome. Your film is financed! You don't have to worry about producing it and doing it all yourself. On the other hand, you're now a director for hire on your own film, which is super cool if you and the producers from the company have the same vision; not so super cool if you don't.

I'm not saying don't go down this route, just that this is the conventional path, and not the "make shit happen on your own" path. As discussed before, only you know what the right way to pursue your movie. Trust your own instincts, and go for it.

STEP 8 CHECKLIST

- ☐ Create an LLC (or get a lawyer to do it for you).
- ☐ Make lists of potential investors.
- ☐ Woo those people with your confidence. Impress them with your package.
- ☐ Collect the checks, and put them in the bank.
- ☐ Be grateful for the journey you are on, and celebrate the fact that you are a bad ass who has just raised the finance you need to make your film.

STEP 9 CROWD-FUND: YOU MUST DO IT!

"If we always helped each
other, no one would
need luck."

SOPHOCLES
Ancient Greek playwright of
Oedipus Rex and *Antigone*

AN ESSENTIAL COMPONENT of your financial plan *must* be crowdfunding (I know some of you are freaking out already . . . but hear me out).

The thing is: It's not just about the funding; it's about the crowd.

The facts of the modern film landscape are that it's very hard to get an audience for your film after you make it. Getting people to watch your film is harder than actually making it. "Build it and they will come" doesn't work anymore (if it ever did).

So the more that you do now to build a crowd for your film, the more likely it is that you will have an audience once you've made it. People who are engaged and invested at an early stage are far more likely to help spread the word when the movie is completed, and unless you suddenly land a huge publicity budget, this is worth its weight in gold.

Years ago, I had a bad impression of crowdfunding, and refused to do it. I thought it was like begging your friends for money. Not dignified, not cool, not in my life. No freaking way.

Since then, I've had a complete paradigm shift in my understanding of it. You're not begging your friends for money, you're giving them the chance to be part of something meaningful. Something awesome. You're not begging at all; you're offering. And they're not donating; they're jumping on board for an adventure. And they don't have to! There's no pressure, and you won't be upset if someone doesn't want to kick some moolah your way. But for those who WANT to, you're giving them the chance to be part of your film, and that can be a very special and generous thing.

Look at it as a way to both raise vital funds for your movie, and build the audience before you start even shooting. You'll see that crowdfunding is totally essential. It's a way to connect your work with an audience before you make the film, and what could be better than that?

The Options

There are two main platforms to choose from:

KICKSTARTER – The granddaddy of crowdfunding platforms. It's Fixed Funding, which means you need to raise 100% of your goal amount to keep any of it. You don't get charged up front, but pay a 5% fee if you are successfully funded. If you don't make your goal, you don't pay anything.

SEED&SPARK – Unique in that it's all about films (i.e., they don't also crowdfund for other things). You need to raise 80% of your target in order to keep the money and pay 2% in fees if your project is successful. S&S also stream movies, and help with distribution.

You might also look into:

INDIEGOGO – They offer both Fixed Funding or Flexible Funding, which means you keep the money you raise, even if you don't meet your target. Like Kickstarter, you pay 5% of your raised funds when the campaign ends, but it's worth noting that they have seriously shifted their attention away from film fundraising recently.

Initially, most people think going with Kickstarter will be the smart choice, because it's the most well-known, hence it will have the most traffic.

It's time for a little myth busting. The people who contribute to your campaign, for the most part, will be people you know. There are not many millionaires surfing Kickstarter, looking for random indie films to kick a few thousand dollars into. It's just not how it works, so it will really be up to you to generate traffic to your campaign page.

I personally used Seed&Spark to raise $35,000 for a movie, and I have to say I couldn't have been happier with the experience. They have a 75% success rate for funding projects (compared with Kickstarter's 37%), and it's for a reason. They get involved, and they help you. They'll tell you if they think your goal is too high, your campaign video ineffective. When your campaign goes live on S&S, it's because they've agreed it's ready, and they think you have a good shot at success. When it comes to crowdfunding, they seriously know their shit.

They are also passionate about creating community, and it's fun to connect with other filmmakers through them. I've made a few friends this way, and I'm grateful for the opportunity to connect with genuinely like-minded filmmakers.

For the record, I am not in any way affiliated with Seed&Spark, and I don't get anything from recommending them. I honestly think they're awesome, and I encourage you to check them out.

Planning your campaign

Just like with your film, the success (or failure) of your campaign is largely set up from your planning or pre-production phase.

You have to be realistic about how much you can raise. You have to do some serious groundwork before you launch your campaign, including making a great campaign video. You have to do your homework, build your email list and plan your social media engagements. You cannot be too prepared.

There are amazing resources out there to help you in this phase.

On a spiritual level, I encourage you to read Amanda Palmer's book, *The Art of Asking*, and watch her TED talk on the same subject. Amanda, a rock star from the band The Dresden Dolls, raised over a million dollars through crowdfunding to record an album. No matter what you think of her or her music, when it comes to crowdfunding she is totally inspirational. If you're having any negative thoughts or fears about crowdfunding, please read her book!

I also recommend you watch the Film Courage interviews with Emily Best from Seed & Spark, which you can find on YouTube. These are more practical, but will help you prepare for what lies ahead.

How much should I aim to raise?

This is the big question, particularly if you opt for a Fixed Funding deal, meaning you only get the money contributed if you reach your goal.

Let's talk about that for a minute—why would you agree to that? Why not take the Flexible Funding offer from Indiegogo and take whatever you raise? In a nutshell: You need a certain amount to make your film happen. If you don't hit the target, will you still be able to make your film? And if you can't make your film, why are you taking money from people?!

There's another reason to go for Fixed Funding, too: It lights a fire under your ass. Nothing will make you work harder to reach your goal than the fact that you won't get any of the money if you don't. For that reason, the percentage of crowdfunders who reach their goal is far higher amongst those who opt for Fixed, rather than Flexible Funding.

Whichever you choose, you still have to set a goal. There are two things you need to ask:

- How much do you need?
- How much can you expect to raise?

For the first question, you might want to break it down. How much do you need to develop your film (i.e., this might even be about raising funds to shoot the concept trailer)? How much do you need to actually shoot your film? How much do you need for post? Also consider how much you think you can raise from private equity (i.e., if your total budget is $100,000, and you think you can raise $80,000 from private equity, consider $40,000 as your crowdfunding goal).

Note that it's perfectly acceptable and possible to run different campaigns for different stages of your filmmaking process. It would also be possible to do those on different platforms, if you wish, so you could do your production cost fundraising on S&S and your post fundraising on Kickstarter.

Now to the second question: How much can you expect to raise?

A good formula, that I learned from Erica Anderson at Seed & Spark, is this:

Take the number of people you have in your immediate network. This includes your Facebook friends, your Twitter followers, your email list, as well as your real world family and friends.

Write that number here:

Five percent of those people will contribute to your campaign. (I know! When I heard that, I thought, "*Come on! More of my friends would contribute than that!!!*" But apparently it's true. Deal with it.)

Write that number here:

The average contribution is $125 (some people will contribute $1000, most will contribute $25, but when you average these out, this what you get). So multiply the last number by 125, and you have a ballpark figure of what you can expect to raise.

Write that number here:

Of course, you can get your key cast and crew to do this too, and add the numbers together, but *only* if they are going to be super involved in the crowdfunding campaign as well.

About This Formula

It makes you realize how important it is to create a network if you're a filmmaker today.

Without any crowd, it's very hard to raise funds.

So, if you're starting from scratch: If you've never made a film before (i.e., you have no audience yet), and social media gives you the heebee jeebees, what do you do?

- Start where you are. Find the social media platform on which you feel comfortable, and start to engage with others there. Your tribe is out there. You need to find them and build it.

- Connect with other filmmakers. Look around on crowdfunding platforms for projects that inspire you. Contribute to them! If you don't have money to do that, share about them on social media.

- Consider starting with a very small crowdfunding campaign to begin the process of building an audience. Don't be over-ambitious.

The fact is: if you want to have a career as a filmmaker today, you need to be willing and able to create a direct connection with your audience.

Look at examples like Ed Burns, Hal Hartley, Ava DuVernay, Shane Carruth, Ana Lily Amirpour, Spike Lee, and Zach Braff and learn from them. They have all successfully crowdfunded their movies. Read interviews with them, and see how they did it. The old model of making movies is dead. Don't be scared of the new.

Crowdfunding Is A Full Time Job

No doubt you've heard this a thousand times before. Don't ignore it. Truly, do not schedule your crowdfunding campaign for a time when you will have no time to work on it.

When I did my last crowdfunding campaign, I thought it would be smart to run it while I attended two film festivals: one in Ashland, Oregon, where I had been invited to teach a workshop; and also to Tribeca where *Bleeding Heart*, my second film, was premiering. I thought the attention that I would get from these would help drive the campaign, as I'd be doing a ton of press at Tribeca, and could mention the crowdfunding every time! The audience in Ashland had loved my first film—getting to talk to them would surely turn into big dollars for my new movie. This thinking turned out to be a huge mistake.

For the four days that I was at the Tribeca Film Festival, I had no time to promote our campaign in my immediate circles . . . and it flatlined. Sure, I was doing press, and talking it up all the time, but no money came in at all. I realized that strangers are not going to read an interview with you in *Indiewire,* and suddenly contribute to your campaign. That's fanciful thinking, and it was borne out by cult director Abel

Ferrarra and Willem Dafoe's attempt to raise $500,000 for a film on Kickstarter. Launched at the Cannes Film Festival, their campaign was covered in every film magazine and website. They couldn't have had more publicity! But still they raised only about $25,000. What went wrong? Clearly, Ferrarra and Dafoe, despite being famous and having fans around the world, weren't connecting with their audience in a personal way. People don't kick in because they liked your last movie. They kick in because they feel connected to you.

The best week in my crowdfunding campaign came the week after I was at the high profile fests. Panicked from the lack of input, and worried that I wasn't going to make my goal, I doubled down on my efforts, and emailed, Facebooked and tweeted shamelessly. I raised $20,000 that week. From this experience, I learned that the only thing that drives a campaign is **you** and the hours you put into it in the circles that know you.

Email lists are gold

Something else I learned: Twitter is good, Facebook is better, but email lists are solid gold.

The conversion rate (i.e., percentage of visitors from a source who actually contributed money) for my campaign was as follows:

Twitter	3.54%
Facebook	9.55%
Rebel Heart Film website	10.71%
My newsletter	21.74%

It's worth pointing out that Facebook still brought the greatest number of contributions, because the reach (compared with my email list) was far greater.

These numbers have made me realize the importance of taking time to build an email list. If your email list had 5,000 people on it, and you managed to maintain a high conversion rate, you'd be in a very strong position indeed when it comes to crowdfunding.

So if you're wondering where you should put your time and energy (growing your email list vs. Facebook vs. Twitter), I think you know the answer.

Connection is key

We've already touched on this, but it's worth mentioning again. You need to build a genuine connection with your tribe. This can't be entirely a one-way flow; it needs to go both ways. If you want people to support you, you need to support other people.

If you don't do it already, start following filmmakers you admire on social media. Browse projects on crowdfunding sites, and follow them. Share information, and promote other people's work regularly through your different channels. It doesn't need to be all about you! Spread the word about campaigns and projects that you think are cool. Your generosity will come back to you a thousand fold, guaranteed. If you help others achieve their dreams, they will be far more likely to help you achieve yours.

Think about NPR (National Public Radio). Most of the time, they are giving you valuable content for free. Then twice a year, they ask for money so they can continue to do that (pledge drives). Your social media presence should be similar—most of the time you should be sharing information of value for free. Information that chimes with your brand as a filmmaker. Then occasionally ask for support. You can't just use these channels to ask for support, as you won't receive it. But if you are regularly contributing something of value, you're far more likely to rake in the money when you need it.

The last word

Allow yourself at least one month to prep your campaign and one month to run it. Try to involve the other members of your cast and crew as much as possible. Ideally, you might take turns leading the campaign, but at the very least, make sure they are all on board and will make a real effort with it as well.

When I launched our campaign, I warned my friends that I was going to be doing it for a month and that there was no pressure for them to contribute, but that I would be very noisy for that time! Most people need to see something at least three times before they act on it on social media, so you have to be relentless. Tweeting once a day and politely sharing on Facebook once a week won't cut it. You have to push, push, and push some more.

It is tough. I won't lie. In fact, initially I found it scary as all hell—easily one of the scariest things I've ever done. I felt vulnerable and very exposed. Here I was asking for help, with no idea if I'd get it. But once it started, I also discovered there is a very beautiful side to crowdfunding. It is humbling, in the most magnificent way, to open yourself to receive support, and to receive it. To check in and see that someone you went to school with decades ago kicked in a hundred bucks. Or that someone you haven't spoken to in years put in twenty. People who you wouldn't expect supporting your dream . . . because you gave them the chance.

STEP 9 CHECKLIST

☐ Plan your crowdfunding campaign.

☐ Launch it, and shamelessly promote the shit out of it.

☐ Be grateful for the journey you are on, and thankful for your awesome network as you hit your goal.

STEP 10
RECRUIT
YOUR CREW

"Employ a strict 'No
 Assholes' policy . . .
 because that [one]
 asshole will ruin your
 movie."

JAY DUPLASS
low budget movie hero, director and actor

ONCE YOU HAVE the money in the bank (at least enough to see you through physical production), you are ready to move into pre-production! Yay!

The first thing you will do is recruit and hire crew.

You've already got a great DP and Line Producer. Who else do you *need*?

Here's a checklist of the key positions that you will be filling:

- First Assistant Director
- Production Designer
- Costume Designer
- Hair/Make-up
- Gaffer
- Grip
- 1st and 2nd Assistant Camera
- Sound Mixer
- PA/runners
- Stills photographer
- Composer
- Editor

Before we go briefly in to each position and what to look for, let's talk about an overall strategy for getting the best crew possible, and getting the best out of your crew.

The Strategy

Send the script to anyone who is interested in working on your film (yep, including P.A.s). Ask them to read it, and then meet with them for a coffee. Talk to them about the script and the film you want to make. Listen to them, and hear their thoughts on it. Do they seem to really get it? Are they excited about it? These are your people.

Some crewmembers are floored by this approach, but I think it's an essential way to get the best out of your crew. You make them feel like a valued part of the team from the start.

On a microbudget movie, if I get a good vibe from a person, I'll say this:

"The truth is thousands of movies get made every year at this budget level, and most of them never get seen anywhere. This movie will probably only ever be watched by our parents. So, if you're just doing this for your career, do another movie.

Obviously you will get paid, but it's not much. You'd make more working at Starbucks. So, if you're doing this for the money, take another job.

But if you love the script, and you like the people who are making it, and you believe we could make a gem of a film if we all work hard, then get on board.

At the minimum, I promise it will be a great experience. We'll all have fun and we'll all get better at what we do."

It's not rocket science: People work best and hardest when they are happy, valued, and feel like they're contributing to something meaningful.

Every person who works on my films brings their A-game every single day. They work their butts off, and have an awesome, creative time doing it.

The way you hire people sets the tone. Your currency as an indie filmmaker is *passion*, and it's passion that will make your film rise above the rest.

So inspire passion in everyone who is going to work on your film, and you stand the best chance to make a truly standout film.

First Assistant Director

I think this is probably one of the single most important hires that you will make, and the one that will determine the success or failure of your film, particularly if you are a first-time director.

The 1st AD runs your set.

They will be responsible for keeping you on time, on budget, on schedule, and safe.

A great 1st AD will be a genius with the schedule. They will have your back 100%, so you will never have to look at a clock while on set. You can do your job, and focus all your attention on the actors and their performances. They will tell you how many more takes you have time for and they will know when it matters (i.e., when it's worth taking ten more takes), likewise they'll know when it's smarter to move along because the shot will probably end up on the cutting room floor. They will keep the crew moving at a good pace.

A great 1st AD will also know all the rules for making your workplace safe. If you have guns on set, they will manage them. They'll be the one who will tell you if you can push into lunch, and what the penalty will be. They'll have a constant sense of where the crew are, and how much you can push them before there's a mutiny.

It's only with previous set experience that a 1st AD can really do their job well, so this is one role where I would strongly encourage you to find someone for whom it's not their first gig. Of course, you could find an experienced 2nd AD who is ready to move up the ladder. Whichever your choose, this person can make or break your film, so make sure you get the right one.

Production Designer

This person is responsible for the on-camera look of your film, which is so important. You can shoot with the fanciest camera in the world, but unless you put something beautiful in front of it, it's going to look like a cheap student film. I should probably repeat that, because it seems so often forgotten. First-time filmmakers are desperate to use expensive cameras that they can brag about to their mates, and then they spend zip on production design. The result? You might have as well have shot it on your phone.

You probably won't have the budget to be building sets, but rather you'll be using real locations and dressing them to suit your film. You need someone who has a great eye and who can do it on a budget; a visionary who knows all the crafty, thrifty ways to make a location pop.

Essential qualities of a Production Designer:
- Great eye
- Shared aesthetics with you
- Local knowledge
- Able to work with your budget
- Resourceful

Costume Designer

A great eye, super contacts, and the ability to shop big on a tiny budget (they better know the thrift stores!) are essential, but if your movie is contemporary, hopefully the actors will also bring a lot of their own clothes to the table.

Your costume designer is not only responsible for designing each look for an actor, but they will also look after the wardrobe during the shoot, laundering the clothes as necessary. Ideally, you want someone who has worked in film before, so they understand about the necessity of doubles in some situations (if there's going to be blood or water, you definitely need at least two sets of identical outfits), and who are super-savvy about continuity.

If you're going for a stylized look for your film, you will want your costume designer and production designer to get together early on so they can coordinate. However, if you want a natural feeling to your film, keep them apart!

Hair and Make Up

Ideally on a microbudget movie, you find one person who can do both of these jobs. However, if your film is all female characters, and you're planning some fancy hair/make-up, you're going to need more. The last thing you want when you're shooting is to be held up because actors are still getting their hair done. So be smart, and plan accordingly.

It depends on the look you are going for in your film, but if you have a very small cast and you want your actors to look natural and real, you might even be able to combine the roles of costume designer and hair/make-up. I've done this on two films, and it's worked perfectly.

Sound Mixer and Boom Boy

Great on-location sound recording is essential if you want to make a standout film.

Sure, you can loop dialogues later with ADR (Additional Dialogue Recording; i.e., recorded in a studio and dubbed), but not only is this expensive and time consuming, it often kills performance.

Make sure you find someone who is passionate about recording great sound. When you are hiring them, make it clear that getting pristine location sound is a priority for you.

If you have the budget, you will also hire a boom boy, i.e., someone to hold the big furry microphone in place (the boom), but it is possible to get someone who will do both.

Gaffer

A gaffer is essentially an electrician who will execute the lighting plan for your film, and I think they are the unsung heroes of filmmaking. I honestly don't think you can underestimate the benefit of an inspired gaffer, not just a technician, but also an artist. They will bring so much to your film and help make it look amazing.

Your DP might have people he or she's worked with, and it is crucial that they get on, so keep your DP in the loop when hiring.

Grip

The grip maintains and builds equipment associated with the camera and with lighting. If you're using any jibs, cranes, dollies, car mounts, not to mention shade structures under a desert sky, it's the grip who will make it happen.

Ideally, you'll have one key grip, perhaps someone who works with the gaffer regularly. Then hire extra hands on days that you anticipate might need them.

Camera Department: 1st and 2nd AC

You'll need at least two camera assistants, and probably a DIT (Digital Information Technician) on top of that.

Typically, your DP is in charge of hiring these positions, and will usually have people she likes to work with.

Script Supervisor

This person is in charge of continuity and coverage (i.e., they will make sure that when you come to edit you have all the shots you need, and they will all match seamlessly). On set, they will also take notes for your editor, for example noting any bad takes, as well as your preferred take.

On my first film, we didn't have a script supervisor. Sheri Davani, my infinitely genius First A.D. said that at our budget level we wouldn't be able to hire anyone any good, and furthermore, if they weren't good, they'd be a pain in the ass and slow us down unnecessarily. She insisted that there was nothing too complicated in our shoot and that we'd be fine. She was right.

If your script is fairly straightforward, and you have production design and wardrobe teams who are continuity savvy, you should be fine. As for notes for the editor, you are probably going to look at every take anyway—no matter what the notes say. Yes, it might make their job a little slower, but no slower than working through notes that are excessive or unhelpful.

It's your call. If you can get someone experienced or really feel you need it, get someone. But it's one position you can probably skip on a very low budget film and not suffer for it.

Still Photographer

Don't for a minute think you can get away without one, because you're good at taking photos and you'll do it. Or the producer will. Or the 2nd AD. Or whoever.

Everyone is so damn busy on a film set, they do not have time to take pictures. You need seriously good pictures. They are 100% essential for when you come to publicize your film, and often a requirement for traditional distribution deals.

So how do you find a still photographer?

I don't think it's essential that the person is experienced in set photography; I do think it's essential that they are good documentary photographers. That they have a great eye, and can work quietly and quickly.

Also, don't skimp and only have them come on certain big days. It's essential that they are there ALL the time, every minute of your shoot. You never know when that ideal poster moment is going to happen, and you'll kill yourself if you miss it.

Production Assistants/Runners

Three words: Pay them something.

They're going to work their butts off, often on thankless tasks like running over to a neighbor's home to ask the gardener please not to use the leaf blower right now! So please give them something for their time.

Treat them well, and make them feel valued.

In addition to these crew positions, you also want to get the following people on board now:

Composer

Don't wait until you've finished shooting to think about music. There is nothing better than working with a composer from an early stage of filming, and let's be clear: Music is one of the strongest aesthetic elements of your film. Don't let it be an afterthought.

We will discuss in detail the role of the composer when we talk about post, but to give you heads up, it's smart to find one now.

Editor

If you didn't find one earlier, you're going to need one now. Don't wait until after shooting to find one because you think editing is part of post-production. Have one on board from the start so that they can be doing rough assemblies even as you shoot.

Also, you might find it helpful for them to make rough assemblies of any scenes that you are concerned about. For instance, if you have a complex multi-shot scene in a certain location, get your editor to do a quick cut of it so that you know you have the scene before you strike the set. It will give you peace of mind, and save you headaches later on.

Final Word

Your crew are the people who will actually make your movie a reality.

Make them happy, and it will be a happy experience.

Choose people who are enthusiastic, hard working, and committed. Inspire them, and give them space to do their jobs. Don't try to micromanage them.

Your crew will grow to be like your family. Let your family be a happy, respectful, functional one; and on that note, if it's not working out with someone, don't be afraid to fire them. You need positive collaborators, and one persistently negative, angry person can ruin it for everyone. Don't let that happen. It's better to get rid of them than let the whole gang get poisoned by one bad apple.

STEP 10 CHECKLIST

- ☐ Assemble the coolest group of inspiring, talented souls you can find.

- ☐ Be grateful for the journey you are on, and celebrate by inviting them all to your house for drinks. Nurture camaraderie.

STEP 11
CAST YOUR
SMALLER
ROLES

"Casting is 65% of
directing."

JOHN FRANKENHEIMER
Old school director of *The Manchurian
Candidate* and *The Birdman of Alcatraz*

THERE'S A SAYING amongst actors: There are no small roles.

Believe it. It's true.

Smaller roles can make or break your movie just as much as the wrong lead, so take time to find the right people.

Push yourself not just to go for the obvious choices. Question what you wrote, and challenge your initial impulses. So often, these will fall into clichés. Consider the fact that only 30% of speaking roles are women. You've grown up watching that, and have ingested it subconsciously, so you will often unwittingly regurgitate it. But does it have to be that way?

Ask yourself: Does the doctor have to be a white man? Could he be black? Asian? Could he be . . . a *woman*?!

As you go through your script and look at each of those smaller roles, turn them inside out, every which way. Don't accept the first picture in your head. Dig deeper and deeper— your film will be so much richer for it.

The importance of time with your actors— *all* of them!

It's absolutely essential to spend some quality time with your actors before you shoot.

You might think: It's a small part, they are an established working actor. We don't need to rehearse or spend time together. They're pros, they'll know what they are doing. We'll figure it out on the day.

Wrong.

If you have a short, tight shooting schedule you do not have time to build a performance from scratch.

I had an experience where a part was cast *after* we had started shooting, meaning I had zero time to rehearse with this actor. It wasn't a huge role—one shooting day—but it was a crucial scene in the film. On the day, the actor, who is super-experienced and undoubtedly talented, showed up, and it was like he was in a different movie. His instincts for the part were totally wrong, but we had a hell of a schedule that day, and there literally wasn't the time to get it right. We just had to shoot and move on. The result? In editing, I cut the scene to its thinnest margin. He is hardly in the completed movie at all.

People who don't know that don't notice it when they watch the movie, but I know what that scene was meant to be, and how it turned out, and the two couldn't be more different. It kills me.

Avoid that disaster, and make sure you get at least one sit-down with *every* actor in your movie before you shoot, so that you can go through their part with them, and make sure they understand what you are looking for *before* they get to set.

Working with non-actors

You might choose, for a number of reasons, to work with non-actors. If the person is right, then it's totally viable.

You have to be creative in finding a way to work with them and get a good performance. You'll have to be patient and resourceful. There is no point in trying to get a non-actor to "act," it will be awful! Instead you have to find a way to allow them to be themselves.

Famously, Andrea Arnold in her film *Fishtank* didn't give

her lead actress (who had never been in a movie before) the whole script. They shot in sequence, and she would only reveal the scene they were about to shoot. Check it out to be inspired!

Also, classic French director Robert Bresson (one of my all-time favorites) regularly used non-actors as his leads. He would get them to repeat a line a hundred times, until they said it with no emotion, no acting . . . and somehow it worked.

In my first film, I cast Rock Novak, a man who lives in a ghost town in the desert of Death Valley, to play himself. He has so much character, you would never find anyone better! There was no way he was going to learn lines and deliver them authentically, so I set up a way of improvising to allow him to be himself. The other actors in the scene knew what was needed and guided the conversations.

Be aware that working in these ways will often take longer than if you are working with an experienced actor, so make sure your schedule allows for it.

STEP 11 CHECKLIST

- ☐ Audition actors for smaller roles.
- ☐ Love those actors. Cast the ones who thrill you.
- ☐ Be grateful for the journey you are on, and thank your actors—all of them.

STEP 12
PRE-PRODUCTION ESSENTIALS

"By failing to prepare, you are preparing to fail."

BENJAMIN FRANKLIN
Founding Father of the good old U.S.A.

YOU HAVE MADE it to the phase we call pre-production. This is when all the war plans are laid in very tight, specific detail. Locations are locked down, permits are attained, parking plans are made, and catering is booked. People are officially hired, contracts are signed.

You are making a movie.

The big thing to say here is: You cannot plan too much.

The success of your shoot is 100% determined in your planning. If you don't do proper groundwork, you have zero chance of making a standout film. If you do it, your shoot should be enjoyable, smooth, and yes, you'll shoot the film you set out to make.

Your line producer (and producers and/or Unit Production Manager) will be working hard during this phase on logistics.

These include:

- **Locking down locations** – Make sure you get signed contracts for each one. Sometimes people agree to let you use their house, store, bar, cinema, whatever, not realizing what it means to let a film crew loose on their property. They freak when they see the trucks arrive, or they freak that night when they come after the first day of shooting and see their house in a wreck! Avoid possible flakers by having it all clearly agreed upon beforehand.

- **Attaining permits** – You may decide to shoot some scenes "guerilla" style (i.e., not get the legally required permit). I get it; I've done it. Decide on strategies if you're not getting a permit: How can you shoot fast, and with least visibility? If the police do approach you, who is going to talk to them, and what are you going to say? Worst-case scenario is your equipment is confiscated, and your set closed down. Don't let it happen to you—plan in advance!

- **Booking required vehicles** (trucks for grip, camera, wardrobe, props)

- **Planning parking for all the vehicles at each location**

- **Planning the catering** – This can be tough on small budgets, because it's so important to feed cast and crew well! Consider "walk-aways" if you are in a city with nearby options, where you give everyone $10, and let them go get their own food.

- **Officially hiring cast and crew, negotiating contracts and dealing with unions**

- **Getting clearances for any brands/book titles/ names/songs/etc. you want to use in the shoot** – Do *not* shoot your lead character singing along to a Rolling Stones song unless you've cleared it (and by the way, that would cost mega bucks, so forget it already unless you're Martin Scorsese and you have an unlimited budget). Typically if you're displaying a brand name, and it's used for its intended purpose, you should be fine. For instance, seeing the Mercedes logo in a car is fine if the character is driving it normally. If the character is drunk driving and hits a kid, you might have an issue. Better in every case to be safe rather than sorry—get everything cleared or don't use it.

- **Acquiring necessary insurance** – Totally essential! *Every* indie shoot needs insurance, trust me.

During pre-production, if you are the director, your job is to mentally prepare for how you are going to shoot each and every scene.

To this end, I recommend four main strategies:

1. **Spend a ton of time with your DP** – I don't think it's necessary to storyboard (i.e., draw pictures of what each and every shot will look like, rather like a comic strip) unless you have a challenging action sequence, but I do think it's necessary to create a shot list. This means discussing each scene with your DP, and coming up with a plan of how you will shoot it. The old-fashioned way often involved drawing diagrams of sets with a pen, but now you can use apps like Shot Designer to help you. Figure out the minimum number of shots you'll need to cover it, plus any bonus shots if you have time when shooting. While in pre-production, share tons of photographs, watch movies together, and discuss the color, composition,

and rhythm of the film you are making. I like to come up with general rules with my DP about how we will shoot the film. With my first film, the rule was: How can we shoot this scene in as few set ups as possible? I wanted it to feel like an older film, with a slower rhythm, and this was one way to achieve that. With my second film, we decided that when the two female leads were together we'd shoot them on a tight axis (i.e., so they're almost looking into the camera when talking to each other) to enhance their connection, while when they talk to other people, we used a loose axis. On set, when under pressure, we would fall back to these rules, and it made our decisions quicker and easier on the fly.

2. **Spend as much time as possible with your actors** – Rehearse, rehearse, rehearse. Does this mean run the lines a thousand times? No, but definitely go through the script in detail with them. Encourage your actors to ask you *anything*. Start building a creative language with them. Make sure that they understand the motivation behind every moment they have, and that they feel confident about every line. Don't wait until you are on set to have these discussions. You want everyone to show up on the day making the same film, and having the same understanding of what a scene is meant to be. During this process, you might make changes to your script—don't be afraid to do that. I'm not Shakespeare, the lines can be changed if the actor

finds a more natural way of saying something. If the actors have a better idea, go with it!

3. **Spend a lot of time at your locations** – This is not obvious, and it's not always possible, but if you can, spend as much time as possible at your locations. Observe the light. Observe the sounds. In your mind, go through all the possibilities for the scene you'll be shooting there. Take pictures. Get excited. Dream.

4. **Go through your script over and over and over** – Keep digging deeper into it. Never stop.

Tech Scouts

A tech scout is when you go to your locations with all your crew, and have a detailed discussion about the logistics of shooting there.

Your line producer or UPM (Unit Production Manager) will be assessing and planning, parking, and catering, as well as where the production crew can set up an office.

Any technical concerns are raised.

A word about this (and it might sound obvious): Don't ignore the concerns!

If your sound guy says it's going to be impossible to get great sound in a location, listen to him. Bad sound will sink your movie quicker than anything.

For this reason, I think the earlier you do preliminary tech scouts the better, so that you don't get attached to a location that just won't work. If there is a location you love and desperately want to use, but it's next to a freeway and sound is going to be impossible, get creative! Don't bullheadedly think you can shoot a dialogue-heavy scene there. Instead consider having the characters walk through this place, but do the talking elsewhere, or shoot them talking from such a distance that looping their dialogue (i.e., dubbing it) won't be a problem. Take a leaf from old B movies and from French films of the *Nouvelle Vague,* and make it work.

Hopefully as you reach your start date for shooting, everything feels planned and prepared. Try to stay calm and rest—you're going to need every ounce of energy for your shoot, so don't burn out early.

STEP 12 CHECKLIST

- ☐ Think about your movie all the time. Dream about it.
- ☐ Spend a ton of time with your actors and your DP.
- ☐ Make sure all the logistics are being taken care of.
- ☐ Be grateful for the journey you are on, and get excited! It's happening. You are making your movie.

STEP 13
GET YOUR
MOVIE IN
THE CAN

"Filming is a funny
combination of having a
good time and not being
able to wait until it's over."

NICOLE HOLOFCENER,
writer/director of *Please Give, Walking
and Talking, Friends with Money*

168 SHOOT FROM THE HEART

THE BIG DAY has arrived: You are going to start shooting. It's an awesome feeling, but daunting too.

You have x number of days to film all the material you need to make your movie.

Hopefully, if you've done the groundwork in preproduction, things should go pretty smoothly.

You'll get to the location in the morning, and be able to park where you planned. Everyone will arrive on time. You'll have the equipment that you need. There will be great food. You'll work hard without interruptions, and capture the scenes you need. It will all be amazing.

But no matter how much prep you've done, shit will happen.

There's no better way to put it.

You can't control everything.

Cameras won't work because it's too hot in the desert. Bees will sleep in their hive, and won't fly around for their shot. An aging ballerina will be sick, and cancel the show you were scheduled to film. A body double, whose only job is to get in the pool for an underwater shot, will reveal that she can't swim. Yes, these all happened to me (and many, many more).

Shit happens, and it happens nearly every day.

It's your job to steer the ship around the icebergs and to make the best decisions that you can at every turn, in circumstances that you can't always anticipate. You have to stop your damn ship from sinking, no matter what.

Ultimately, a film is quite simply the sum of the choices you make when making it. So you need to be in the zone and make great choices on the fly.

You're making a movie, not shooting the script.

This is a big thing to remember.

Your job is not just to make the day and get the pages done. Your job is to make an awesome movie. So, while it's vital that you keep your foot on the pedal and make your days, it's also vital that you keep your eye on the bigger picture.

A lot of first-time directors get stuck because they try to adhere too strictly to the plan. By trying to capture the movie in their heads, and trying to film the script, they drive themselves crazy trying to force it to be something that they can't capture.

It's like a Zen Koan: On the one hand, you've got this great script and this terrific shot list and plan, and if you don't get it in the can each day, you're screwed. On the other hand, if you try to stick to the plan, even when it's not working, and you aren't open to what is happening in the moment, you're also screwed. In fact, it's having the awesome plan that makes it possible to be free.

The biggest advice I can give you for your shoot, if you want to make a standout film, is be fully present in the moment when you are filming.

Do not be attached to the plan.

Let lotus flowers grow from the shit that happens.

Turn your obstacles into advantages.

Be startlingly awake. Notice magic when it's happening, and drop the plan so you can capture it. Nine times out of ten, it will be far better than what you had imagined.

Let me give you an example. If you've seen the Oscar-winning film *Moonlight*, you probably remember the beautiful scene where a drug dealer teaches a young boy to swim in the ocean. There are no lines in it, it's purely visual, and it's an incredible cinematic moment—absolutely transcendental, the kind of magic we all seek. Turns out it wasn't planned that way. In the script, there was a dialogue-heavy scene between the two characters. But a storm was closing in, which meant they had two hours to shoot the scene (instead of six). Furthermore, the water was so choppy, the DP couldn't keep the camera above the water. The result is the most memorable moment in a film filled with them.

It's one of the greatest blessings of making a small movie: You can change your plan in a minute. You don't need to go to your financiers and producers and ask permission. Unlike big studio films, you're not filmmaking by committee, and this gives you a huge advantage when it comes to making a standout film.

You can adapt and go with the flow, and capture the film as it presents itself to you in the moment.

Getting the best from your actors

Let me start this by saying that many things in your film can be below par, and some people will still dig it. Your film might be sloppily shot, or the sound might not be perfect. There might be continuity errors or mismatching in the lighting; and amazingly the audience will forgive all of these things if, and only if, they are engaged by the story. And to be engaged by the story means they believe in the characters.

The one thing that absolutely has to be spot on, and this is non-negotiable, is the actors' performances. If the acting is bad, your film is bad. Period. Doesn't matter if it's shot beautifully, or the lighting is amazing, or the costumes are breathtaking. None of it matters if the acting isn't perfect. Consequently, your number one priority at all times on set has to be getting the performances right. In a way, nothing else matters.

So how do you do it?

The first thing to know is that every actor is different. They have different methods, and different input will help them get where they need to be. If you've cast well, sometimes you'll find all you have to do is let them get on with it and stay out the way! If that's the case, you are very lucky—enjoy it.

In any case, if you took your time to rehearse (and you seriously should), you will already have some idea how of they work. Once you get to set, you'll get an even better idea. On your first day with any actor on set, pay extra close attention to them. Do they tire easily? Do they like to chat with crew, or do they need space? What makes them tick?

Some actors are amazing on their first couple of takes then burn out; others need to do a few takes to warm up and get better and better. If you find you've got one who knocks it out of the park on the first take but then just dials it in, reverse the usual idea of wide master shot first, and start with their close up. Your DP might resist this but there's no point in wasting an Oscar-worthy performance on a master shot that you won't use. Also, when you go to do close-ups, start with the actor who you feel has the tendency to burn out quicker.

A director's job on set is quite simply is to be a bullshit detector. That's what it boils down to. No one else on set is doing that, just you. Your DP is making sure the shot is in focus and well composed, your hair/make-up artist is checking for shine on an actor's face or flyaway hairs. The crew are all watching the monitor intently to make sure that their work is flawless, so the thing you need to watch for is that every moment feels true; that your actors are believable and that they are delivering the performances that will make the film fly.

For that reason, I strongly believe that you should stay as close to your actors as possible when you're shooting. It's become common to set up a monitor (often in another room) where everyone huddles to watch what is being shot (a.k.a. "video village"). Very often these days, that's where you'll find the director. To me, this is a huge mistake. Obviously, when your DP is setting up a shot, you should check the monitor to make sure you love it, but then I recommend staying close to the camera when the scene is actually being shot, and watching the actors live.

Part of this is because when you call cut, an actor always instinctively looks to you for direction, and you need to be there. Who else are they going to turn to? They need to know if they're hitting the right note, and you need to be there to guide them. Often, you can keep things flowing and not break the spell. You don't need to shout "Cut!"; you can whisper it, quietly give some directions to the actor and then go straight back to action. Maintaining the mood of the scene is key.

The bottom line is actors are like children (I'm sure a few of them would like to shoot me for saying that, but seriously, it's true), and you are like the parent. You need to foster a relationship of total trust with them. In order for them to let down their guard and do inspired work, they have to feel completely safe and protected, and it's your job to do that.

So be there for them; be close, be present. Watch for truth.

If you are having a totally stressed day on set (your producer is being an asshole, you're running out of time, the hero's car has been in an accident; in other words: your movie is screwed!!!) here's what you do: You do not let the actors know there is anything wrong. When they ask you, "Do you think we'll make our day today?" and in your mind you think, "There's no freaking way we're going to make our day—ARE YOU NUTS?!," you just flash them a Zen smile and reply, "Sure! Of course we're going to make it! It's going to be great."

Protect them. Just like children who don't need to know that the world is falling apart, lie and make them feel safe. That is your job. Whatever they need to deliver a cracking performance, you need to provide.

On that note, it's quite common on indie films to joke about A-listers and their fancy-ass Winnebagos, while these actors make do with nothing. Here's the deal: Actors need some place that's quiet and private to prepare for their scenes. It's not a luxury. After their hair and make up is done, and their costume is on, they need a sanctuary where they can prepare for the scene while the gaffers and grips do their work getting a shot ready. Don't make them wait by the craft service table, chatting to PA's. It's not fair. If you want great performances, seriously don't do it. Make sure that in each location you have a good space designated for them.

Value your actors, and do whatever you can to create the

situation where they will be able to give their best to the film. When they're on set, be in the moment, be responsive and alert to their energies and talents, and make sure you are doing everything you can to make sure they are doing their best work.

Truly: Nothing else matters.

How to get the best from your crew

Feed them well – Good food will make them happy and feel valued; crappy food will set them all complaining and make them slow.

Treat them well – Be respectful and appreciative. Notice their good work, and thank them for it. Also, keep them safe. No shot is worth someone getting injured for (more on this later).

Keep things moving along – Nothing brings crew morale down faster than them thinking that they're not making the days.

Work hard, be positive, and lead by example.

It's pretty much that simple.

One other thing: If you're a first-time director, you will be surrounded with people who are way more experienced at being on set than you. Don't be a jerk and pretend that you know it all. Nothing annoys experienced crew more than a

The cast and crew of Obselidia; a happy family even after ten days in the desert.

first-time director who acts like they know exactly what they are doing while basically screwing up all the time.

Be big enough to trust the people around you. Ask questions. Lean on their expertise. Never be afraid to say you don't know something. When an argument about eyelines breaks out between your first AD and your DP, be honest and say you don't know what an eyeline is (by the way, if that argument does come up, settle it by filming it both ways, and you'll be covered!) Be honest, authentic, and appreciate their knowledge. They'll appreciate it from you.

Even so, just like with your actors, show confidence every day. If inside, you're thinking *"Holy shit, we are never going to make this day, this movie is a freaking disaster!"*—try not to show it. Exude a sense of everything being under control at all times.

You are the captain of the ship, and the crew like to feel like they're in good hands. That you know where they're heading and you've got their back. No one wants to be on a sinking ship, so don't let them have that impression, even if on some days you're sure as hell you've hit the iceberg.

On that note, this might be obvious, but it's always worth highlighting: safety is everything.

To me, this isn't just about staying within the law and using common sense when you are shooting (like, please: No stolen shots on live railways. Ever.).

It's also about respecting your crews' need to rest and sleep. Stay within your days, and make sure everyone gets proper turnaround. Don't let people drive home in the dark after shooting for seventeen hours. It's not fair, and it's not safe.

At the end of the day, it can be said that all that matters is what's on the screen. However, what is on the screen will be so much better if the people who are making it happen are happy, well fed, and safe.

Your team will also be happier if you follow this simple rule:

Don't be a micro-manager

You have surrounded yourself with a team of terrific, talented people. If you've done that, your job should be fairly easy now.

Good sound will be recorded. Great images will be captured and properly stored with back ups. Amazing performances will be delivered.

Everyone will be doing their job—and as much as possible, you just need to stay out of the way and let them do it. You are overseeing the big picture, so you don't have to obsess about every little one. Trust your crew, and let them do their jobs. They will thank you for it by doing their best work—and that's what will make your movie amazing.

However, if you hear someone on set say "We'll fix it in post!," don't believe them.

Two words: *you won't.*

I'm not trying to be a party-pooper, but unless you have a huge budget, it's seriously not going to happen. Make sure you get what you need on the day.

Make sure you get great, clean sound. Listen to your sound guy when he says you need to hold (sure, it can be a pain in the butt, but a bigger one is not being able to use a great take because the sound is a dud). If you are having a bad day with sound problems (i.e., buses keep thundering by) and you really have to move on, make sure that you get every line clean at least once.

Make sure the boom is out of the picture frame at all times, and that the focus puller knows what they are doing.

Always make time to get room tone. It's essential.

Also, if there are some lines you need that are not being filmed (say for example, a message left on the phone), record them during a lunch break.

Have a plan if you have many dialogue-heavy scenes in cars. Consider stealing a shot used in old B-movies where the camera is in the backseat, you can see where the car is going, and the eyes of the driver are in the rearview mirror. It's a super effective shot, and you can dub in any dialogue you want later, very easily, as you can't see the driver's mouth.

Also, rather than wait until ADR sessions months later, record the dialogue lines in the car when it's stationary during a lunch break. It's so much better to get the actors to record the lines there, while they're in character, than it is to get them to do it months later when they've forgotten what the scene was about. You'll also have lines to work with immediately in the edit, and won't have to dub in temp lines (likely recorded by you and your editor) while you wait to get the real ones from a studio session.

I cannot stress enough how much better it is to get live sounds in your locations if possible, rather than "fixing in post." Real live sounds will elevate your movie and give it organic life, rather than deadening it with generic library sounds and ADR recorded months later.

Make it a priority to get what you need every day, and you'll make your editing process so much better.

The final word on shooting: Enjoy it!

The shoot is one of the most intense times of your film-making process, but it's also one of the most fun. It is true that you have the pressure of a ticking clock every single day, but you also have a talented team of amazing, creative people working together to make your film a reality. The feeling of a single purpose amongst such a gang has to be one of the best in the world. When it's all going good, nothing is better.

But even if it's not going exactly the way you hoped, don't turn it into a stress party. No one's going to die if you don't get that shot. You're not at war, you're not curing cancer. You're making a movie.

It's a privilege to be doing it; one you should be infinitely grateful for every day. When approached like that, it's also a joy.

If you make your film in that spirit, with an open, joyful, grateful heart, appreciative of everyone around you, I guarantee you'll have a better chance of success with your film. It won't be birthed from fear and ego; it will come from somewhere pure, and that is the ultimate secret ingredient that makes certain movies more than the sum of their parts. Magic.

Enjoy!

STEP 13 CHECKLIST

- ☐ Show up on time.
- ☐ Work your butt off every day.
- ☐ Treat everyone with kindness and respect, and let them do their jobs
- ☐ Don't get stressed.
- ☐ Be grateful for the journey you are on, and thankful to the souls who are on it with you. Appreciate your privilege, and enjoy every minute of it.

STEP 14
POST
PRODUCTION
ESSENTIALS
EDITING, MUSIC,
COLOR, SOUND

"The end of a picture is
always an end of a life."

SAM PECKINPAH
director of *The Wild Bunch, Straw Dogs*
and *The Getaway*

YOU MADE IT through your shoot, and your film is now ready to be born.

Although you can't fix it in post, your film will be rewritten from the ground up in this phase. You have the rough material, but now is when you shape it into something special.

You cannot underestimate the effect of the work and choices you will make here, in the edit, in the sound mix, in the music and in the color correction.

A so-so movie could become spectacular with the right choices. A good movie could sink with bad ones.

So again, make sure that the creative team you choose to work with is inspired and excited by your vision. It will make all the difference.

The Edit

Ideally, as you were shooting, your editor was at work, getting to know all the footage, organizing it, and making rough assemblies of the scenes. These assemblies will use all the set-ups you shot (i.e., if you shot a master, and two singles, it will use each of these, though you may end up choosing to use only one or two of your options). The editor won't be making big creative choices at this point, but rather will be sticking close to the script and selecting either takes you marked as your preferred ones during the shoot, or the ones that seem best to him or her.

After you finish the shoot, please do catch up on sleep for a few days and decompress. Once you've got a clear head, join your editor, and view what they've put together. If they've been working diligently since the start of the shoot, they might even already have an assembly of most of the film for you to watch.

Now you get to see, in the cold light of day, what you've got to work with. It may not be what you thought. It's time to get really objective and honest about what you do have, and to be willing to take the plunge to write your movie again.

If you want to make a standout movie:
- Do not be attached to your script.
- Do not be attached to scenes or moments because they were difficult to film.
- Do not be attached to any of it.

Be totally dispassionate and honest about what is serving your story and what isn't.

The film might change a lot at this point. You might find one character just isn't working. Be creative, and find ways to bring their screen time down. Or you might find one performance is dynamite. Dial up the screen time.

You may find you have a sub-plot with whole scenes that don't feel necessary, and this may not even be because they are bad. With my first film, there was a whole thread about the lead character's father who had Alzheimer's. At script stage, it seemed to strengthen one of the main themes of the film; the power of forgetting vs. remembering. It also gave the lead character a strong backstory and helped explain his obsession with remembering. We shot the material, and it was great. The guy we cast to be his Dad was really special, totally heartbreaking. The scenes were lovely.

Then in the rough cut, the film was feeling slow, and those moments just seemed to drag it down. I realized that this movie wasn't a story about a guy healing his relationship with his Dad. It was the story of a man coming to terms with his own mortality. The stuff with the Dad was just distracting. It also felt overdone. It was such a big thing, a scene with a father who doesn't know his son. It was beautiful, but it unbalanced the rest of the movie.

So, with a heavy heart, we took it out. It hurt, because I loved it—but it was the right decision for the film. You've probably heard the line, "to be a screenwriter, you have to be willing to kill your babies." It's totally true, you do often have to cut scenes or lines of dialogue that you think are the best things you've written. The thing about being a screenwriter, though, is you can always resurrect them in another script if they really are that good! But it's hard when you're editing, and you know how much work went into shooting a scene. This is why it's important to have an editor who is totally objective working with you.

The story is everything. If it doesn't serve it, cut it.

When is the film finished?

There is a saying that a film is never finished, it's just abandoned. It's heartbreaking, but in many ways, it's true.

You could work on your edit forever, but you shouldn't. There will come a time when, if you keep working on it, it will be overcooked.

More than likely, after you've done the first assembly, you will go through the whole film again twice, scene by scene, moment by moment. I usually like to work sequentially, starting at the beginning and moving through the scenes in order. Pay attention to everything. Make sure you are always using the best takes of the actors, and that every moment feels true.

Once you have gone through the whole thing at least twice, and you are starting to feel confident about it, add some music if you haven't already, and get your editor to tidy up sound as much as possible.

Then I recommend organizing a small test screening. For this, you don't need more than ten people. Six or eight is great. Try to think who the ideal audience is for your movie, and make sure at least a couple of the people you invite fall into that category. Then bring them to your home, give them popcorn and a glass of wine, and show them your movie.

Before it starts, explain to them that the sound isn't done yet, and nor the color. Most people aren't used to seeing a movie in this raw state, and it can jar them, but getting their reactions is still going to be incredibly helpful.

The fact is, at this point, you are way too close to the material to be a good judge of it. You need fresh eyes, and that's what your friends will provide.

After the movie is finished, you can get them to write down responses, though I prefer just a good informal chat. It's worth noting that usually just from the experience of sitting in a room with people watching the film, I already know the changes I want to make. You can feel when an audience is into a film, when you've got them, just as you can sense when you've lost them. Be aware of your thoughts as you watch it with them. If you're thinking if we can just get past this scene,

I know they're going to love it ... that scene is a problem! You need to work on it.

Even though I've already got a pretty clear idea of what I need to work on just by watching it with them, it's fun and helpful to have a discussion. There are a few questions that I always ask, and that I think are most important:

1. **Did you understand everything? Was there anything in the story that wasn't clear to you?** – This is crucial. Unless you're deliberately trying to confuse the audience (David Lynch, take a bow), you want them to understand the story. Sometimes you think it's clear, but it isn't. You need to know this.

2. **How did you find the pace? Any area where you felt bored? Lost interest?** – Ask this, even though during the screening you can usually tell where you've lost them (they start fidgeting), because it's crucial. Pace is everything; even with a deliberately slow film, you want to make sure that the audience stays engaged.

3. **What did you feel the movie was about?** – Here's where I see if what I think it's about is coming through—and I'm often surprised. I might discover things I hadn't realized about it. This question helps me see the film better from an audience's perspective.

4. **How did you feel about the main characters? Did you care about them? Did you understand them? Was there anything they did that you didn't believe?**

I care less about whether people *like* a character, and more about whether they *believe* the character and are engaged by the character's journey.

5. **What was your favorite scene or moment in the film? What was your least favorite?** – Again, it helps me see the film from an audience's perspective, and that helps me make decisions in the editing room.

Also, there might be very specific questions pertaining to the cut of the movie that you need to ask. For instance, you might ask if they understand why Jack phoned his grandma at the end, or how Sally got from London to LA (or if it mattered!). Anything that you are questioning in the editing room, this is your chance to bring it out.

Just like with script notes, you'll get some random feedback that you can ignore, but if *everyone* says they were falling asleep at the forty-five minute mark, you need to do something about it. Don't ignore what they are saying or be overly precious about your work, as hard as it can be. Yes, you are the author (or *auteur*), but at the end of the day, a movie is made to be watched. If people are not responding the way you hope, you have to be honest about that, and try to fix it while you still have the opportunity.

So, now armed with their notes and fresh insight, it's time to go back to the editing room for another round of changes.

How long does this process go on for?

If your movie doesn't have any major problems (i.e., the performances are all essentially solid, you have decent footage for every scene and altogether it's working), I think three months is plenty.

Two months to get to the first cut (the one you first share with friends), then one more month for tweaks (during which, feel free to have further screenings if you find them helpful).

Then one day, when you feel happy about every moment in the film, when you feel it is the best representation of the movie with the footage you had, you say "done," and you *lock picture*.

Locking Picture

It's a big deal when you lock picture, so don't do it until you feel really sure this is it. Once you lock, and the film is "turned over" for sound and color work, it's a headache (not to mention it costs $$$) to go back and change things.

If there is no particular time pressure (i.e., no festival deadline pressing down on you), leave it for a couple of weeks before you lock. Then watch it again, and make sure there are no further changes you want to make.

You want to be 100% confident you've got the best cut possible when you say to your editor, "let's turn it over."

The Score

THE CONVENTIONAL WAY: While you are editing you lay in temporary tracks, pop songs and bits of score grabbed from other soundtracks, to use as a guide. Then once you've locked picture, you hire a composer and get them to compose a score copying those cues.

THE REBEL HEART WAY: You engage a composer *before* you start editing, perhaps even before you shoot (maybe even before you did your concept trailer!). The composer provides pieces of music that inspire you while you work.

As you edit, your composer responds to the cuts you send, and gives you more music to work with. It's an organic, two-way process. The music is informing the cut, and the cut is inspiring the music.

By the time you lock picture, your composer is far into having all the elements lined up, and now it's just a matter of synching them to the final edit.

It's such a better way of working. Of course, it means you need a composer who's willing to invest some real time with you, and who wants to do inspired work (not just replicate some temp tracks for a quick buck). Those composers are out there, and it is seriously worth your time and energy to find one.

With my first film, I reached out to an old friend of mine, Liam Howe, after I had made the concept trailer. Liam was in a pop band, The Sneaker Pimps, and works non-stop as a music producer for the likes of Lana Del Rey and Ellie Goulding. He jumped at the chance of getting to score a film; something that had always been a dream of his.

For the concept trailer, I used some classical music, Glenn Gould playing Bach's The Well Tempered Klavier. Liam came up with the idea of basing the entire score on that piece of music. He also developed the idea of making the whole score out of obsolete instruments, as the film is about obsolescence. He recorded the first piece of score (ultimately used in the opening titles) long before we shot the film. In fact, I listened to it constantly as I did rewrites of the script, and played it on set to create the right mood. Liam's vision inspired our on-set sound mixer, Tom Curley, to grab recordings of any special sounds we came across as we filmed, like the bell wheel in the Museum of Jurassic Technology.

Liam's vision didn't just inspire our sound mixer; it inspired me! This is the best thing about working with a composer early on. Music is so crucial to creating the mood and tone of your film, getting it right early can help you hone the feeling you're going for.

Regardless of whether you plan to hire a composer before shooting or not, don't wait until you're in post to think about the soundtrack. Plan ahead.

For instance, you might be thinking that you don't want a score. Rather, you want to use pop songs like Tarantino does. That's cool and it's your aesthetic choice, but one thing to be aware of: this can be a very expensive route to go down. Prohibitively so for most small indies, if you are hoping to use known tunes by famous artists.

To give you an idea: Initially with *Obselidia*, we did lay in two pop tracks as temps. One was over the montage when Sophie and George drive out to the desert for the first time. It was by a rather obscure band called Clap Your Hands Say Yeah!. The second was over the end titles, it was an acoustic version of a song from the 80's called *It's a Wonderful Life* by Black. Note that neither of these are as famous as, say, The Rolling Stones or Beyoncé.

In the end, we fell in love with these songs in those spots. This is the eternal danger with temps! Liam felt that to write songs to replace them was going to be really hard. When the film got into Sundance, we decided to pay for festival rights to those songs. This cost about $1800. We figured we'd deal with it later. Maybe we would get lucky, sell the film and whoever bought it would pay licensing! The dream, right?!

The film didn't sell, and when we finally came to release the movie ourselves over a year later, we had to go back and deal with it. We couldn't afford the $5,000 it would have cost to buy the rights to both songs, plus it just didn't make sense to raise more money for it at that point.

So, we got Liam to compose a piece for the montage, and we discovered it really worked. Then we sweet-talked our sound mixer into opening the files and dealing with it. He also inserted the meditation bell sound that I decided to use over the end titles in place of the song.

I would never again go to a festival with music in my film that we had only festival rights to. It's the music equivalent of "we'll fix it in post." You're just creating a headache for later. If you can't afford it now and for eternity, don't wait. Find the solution now.

Let's also dispel a common fantasy: *I'll reach out to the artist directly, and they'll love the movie and cut me a deal.*

Hey, it might happen. But realistically, probably not. That's because often the artist doesn't even own all the rights to the song, and you have to deal with the publishers. So even if the artist is very sympathetic, it might not happen.

Of course, try it if you feel in your heart it's the perfect fit. You have nothing to lose, and you just never know (*never say impossible!*), but be smart and have a backup plan in place.

Another option is to find unsigned bands or artists, and work with them. You may find that they will be willing to license tracks to you for a reasonable sum.

The next stages

Once you've locked picture, there is no hard and fast rule about the sequence of finishing your film.

The sound mix and color correction could happen concurrently. Some people swear by completing color first and then doing sound. Others prefer getting the final sound mix done first, so you can watch and correct color with the proper sound.

Certainly, one might affect the other. If, for instance, you have a scene that you want to be scary, you might find after you've done the color and made it super dark and spooky, it really doesn't need much sound work to sell it. Alternatively, if you've done the sound mix first, you might find that making it so dark is over-egging it. There definitely is a balance.

One thing I will recommend is this: If at all possible, hire a post production supervisor.

In my experience, every time you move files, some mishap happens. And it's never clear who is responsible, and everyone passes the buck (the sound mixer blames the color correctionist, who blames the editor). It's a total headache, and unless you are a tech-wizard, you have zero idea of how the problem arose, never mind how to solve it.

In addition, actually moving the drives around, and coordinating the schedules for getting things done is a specific and time-consuming job.

A post-production supervisor understands all the tech aspects, has relationships with the post houses, and is responsible for it all happening according to schedule.

If you can't afford a post supervisor, I recommend trying to find a facility that can do both sound and color. This way you're going to minimize the problems encountered when moving files from one location to another.

One other thing: Don't think you can jump these steps and make a standout movie. Great sound and color are absolutely crucial, and are two of the obvious elements that separate amateur films from professional films. You *must* do a professional sound mix and color correction. It's when your movie becomes a movie.

Sound Mix

What happens in a sound mix?

First, you'll do a spotting session with your mixer, and possibly a dialogue editor, and mark any places of special concern.

You'll decide where you need to use ADR (Additional Dialogue Recording), for which your actors will come into the studio and re-record any lines that are unusable, as well as any voiceovers and additional lines you want to add off camera.

You'll also make a plan for general sound tones and notes. You'll discuss the feeling/mood of each scene and how to help create it with the sound palette.

To clean up scenes that were recorded outside, sometimes the best strategy is to add noises, and you'll discuss what those might be (adding sounds of crickets, dogs barking, distant sirens, etc.).

After that, the sound mixer will get to work gathering all the sounds necessary to make the final sound mix. They'll probably work with a foley artist to record some things (i.e., the sound of footsteps or a door creaking open), and then they'll bring in the actors to record the ADR. The other thing you'll need to be present for is the ADR session, so that you can direct the actors and make sure you get the performances that you're looking for.

Once the sound mixer has all the elements ready, you will join them to do the final sound mix. This will probably take at most a week.

My own feeling about ADR is the less you need to use, the better. Actors coming into a studio months after shooting and trying to recapture the quality of performance they gave . . . it's not easy. Even for real pros. There's often something fake about it.

You can sense it in a film. Often if you're watching a movie and wondering why a scene doesn't gel, why it doesn't ring true . . . it's ADR, that's why. So, unless you need it because the location sound is truly unusable, I recommend sticking with the performances you have.

Color Correction

What can happen in color correction is nothing short of a miracle. Not only can you change the entire mood and look of your film, but you can get rid of something on the screen that bugs you, you can make your actors look more gorgeous than they did on the day, turn a green door into a red door . . . truly anything is possible (if you have the time and the money!).

Even with fairly basic work, this is when your movie starts to really look like one. Along with the score, it ties it all together thematically and gives it the right mood. If you think your movie looked okay before the color correction, you'll be blown away by how it looks afterwards.

VFX

Another thing to mention here is VFX (visual effects).

If your film is a contemporary drama or comedy, you probably won't need to do any. If you need just one or two minor things (i.e., changing the message on a cell phone, or adding stars to a night sky shot to make it pop), you might find that, between your editor and your color correctionist, you're covered, so check with them first.

If it's a bigger job than they can handle (brains being blown out of someone's head, for example), you'll need to find a VFX technician. However, if you have a bigger job, ideally you would plan it *before* you shoot. You'll need to budget for it, and it's also worth discussing that kind of work with your VFX person before shooting, so you make sure you get the material they will need to make it work.

Credits

The end credits and final lay off can both be done by your color correctionist.

Be aware that when it comes to credits there may be contractual duties, so make sure you honor them.

It's totally a matter of taste if you want them to play before the movie or at the end, but be conscious about the effects of your decision.

It's become very modern to have few titles at the start of the film; often you'll just see the film company's name, and then the film starts. This throws the viewer into the film, and can enhance the feeling of the action being "real." It takes away the theatricality of the experience.

Older movies, however, tend to have long credit sequences at the beginning of the film, and if you go back to the thirties or forties, you'll see that there's really no credits at the end (just a title card saying THE END).

With my first film, I knew I wanted it to feel like an older movie, so I went for an extended credit sequence at the beginning. With my editor, John-Michael Powell, I made jpegs of the title cards, and then had them made into old-fashioned slides. After that, we fired up the old slide machine, projected them, and filmed the slideshow, into which I incorporated vintage slides (that belonged to our production designer) and photographs I had taken. Through this, the theme and tone of the film are introduced.

The key, as with everything: Don't wait until now to think about it! Have a plan from the start. Observe carefully how other films handle the credits, as it really can be a powerful method of strengthening the world of your film. Nothing should be left to chance in your film including these.

Letting go

After you've done the credits, you are finished.

It's such a strange feeling after all those months, or possibly years, of focused work. Not many people talk about it, but I often feel a strong sadness at this point. I may love the film that I've made. I may feel incredibly disappointed by some of it; but no matter what, it's hard to let go.

Don't be surprised if you feel this way. Hopefully when you watch it, regardless of its flaws, you will feel a real sense of achievement. You should. You did it. *You* made your film. You made it happen, and no matter what comes next, you should be proud of yourself. Millions of people dream of making a movie, but you actually did it.

Give yourself some time to decompress if you need it. The hard thing is by this point, you're often broke and quickly need to get another job to keep paying the rent. Nonetheless, make an effort to replenish yourself, however that looks for you. You've climbed a giant mountain, but you've got a bigger one ahead of you...getting people to watch your movie.

STEP 14 CHECKLIST

- ☐ Edit until you have the best film possible.
- ☐ Lock picture.
- ☐ Score the film.
- ☐ Arrange sound and color correction, and be prepared for your movie to become a REAL MOVIE.
- ☐ Sweat over the credits (should your mom get Thanks, Special Thanks or Very Special You-Are-A-God Thanks?!).
- ☐ Be grateful for the journey you are on, and cry when it's finished, but remember that you'll get to do it all again.

STEP 15
SUBMIT TO FESTIVALS

"Be with those who help
 your being."

RUMI
13th century Persian poet and mystic

NOW IT'S TIME to launch your movie into the world, and there's no doubt that one of the best ways of doing that is to premier it at a festival. Of course, this path is not always easy, and it can take a lot of work and patience. It can be frustrating. You might feel like you are giving up control, as you are relying on a gatekeeper (a festival programmer) choosing your film. This is all true, but what is also true is that with a very limited publicity and marketing budget (if you have any at all), getting the boost from a well-regarded festival could be a game-changer for your film and your career.

So where should you start? Which festivals should you gun for? The answers to these questions will totally depend upon the film you have made. It's certainly true that all festivals are not created equal. Besides having different levels of prestige, they each have their unique characters. So, before you start spending big bucks on festival entry fees, do your homework. Don't waste your time submitting to fests that are never going to take your film in a million years.

That doesn't mean don't aim high. A rule of thumb, start with the fests that are the most prestigious and the hardest to get into, then work down from there. The top-tier fests generally won't consider your film if it has already premiered somewhere else, so don't blow your world premier on a small local fest if you think you have a legit chance of getting into Toronto.

The top-tier festivals:
Toronto
Cannes

Berlin
Venice
Sundance

These fests are also film markets, and are without doubt the highest profile launching pads for movies. All the major distributors will be at these looking for films to buy, along with all the press. If your film gets into one of these, you have essentially won the filmmaking lottery.

The second tier arguably includes (in no particular order):
Tribeca
SXSW
Rotterdam
Telluride
Edinburgh
Karlova Vary
San Sebastian

These festivals are exceptionally well respected, and you are certainly guaranteed good press, if not the same sales opportunities of the top tier fests.

Next:
There are a ton of excellent regional film fests, which include (but are in no way limited to):
Los Angeles
Palm Desert
London

Ashland

Seattle

And many more . . .

The best of these are extremely worthy: well organized, well curated, attracting a reasonable amount of press attention. All in all, good regional festivals are a fantastic way for a film-maker to connect their film with an audience and launch it to the world.

The bad ones (and there are bad ones out there) are just a plain waste of time and entry fee. They don't carefully curate their films, and don't seem to care about connecting them with an audience. The result? Empty theaters and no buzz. Pointless.

So seriously, do your homework. I know one filmmaker who spent nearly $3000 on festival entries. I watched her film, and I could have told her that she didn't have a chance at most of them, not because her film wasn't any good, but because it didn't fit with the style of most of these festivals.

Take time to research online. Look at what they pro-grammed in previous years. Does your film fit the mold? Ask other filmmakers about their experiences; were they well looked after? Was there a large audience for their movie? Never assume that because a festival is in a cool town it must be a cool festival—I've made this mistake. Don't do it!

Specialist Festivals

Aside from regional festivals, there are special interest fes-tivals; for example, there are festivals specifically for horror

Film families are the best: with Joanne Feinberg at the Ashland Independent Film Festival

movies, LGBTQ audiences or films by women. These can be great, because they really hone in on a niche audience, and that can be perfect for your film. Don't think that you are limiting your movie by playing it in one of these fests. You might think everyone will love your film, but really you want to focus your marketing on a particular audience, and these fests will give you access to that.

Of course, you might be asking if you *need* a festival premier at all, and that is a fair question.

If you're hoping to sell your film to a distributor or to a streaming company like Netflix or Amazon, a premier at a top festival will seriously increase your chances of that happening.

But even if you're planning to distribute your movie yourself (hence you're not seeking a buyer), there's no doubt that a good festival can help you get some good press attention and create some buzz. If you handle those well, that can result in increased sales of your film. If you choose to play in further festivals, it's a continued way to increase visibility of your film on someone else's dime and organization.

One other thing: Festivals are an awesome way to connect with other filmmakers and grow your network. You might meet future collaborators. At the very least, you get to hang out with your filmmaking tribe, compare stories from the battlefields, and talk movies nonstop! In other words: super fun and nourishing for filmmakers who are often working alone.

Finally, in some ways, they're the equivalent of a live gig for filmmakers. There's nothing better than sitting in a dark theater with a crowd of people watching your movie, and having the chance to answer their questions afterwards. Not only is it rewarding in itself, it's an opportunity to really learn and grow as a filmmaker.

Of course, you don't *need* a film festival to make this experience happen. If you want, you can four wall theater space (i.e., rent it) and create your own premier experience. Alternatively, if you don't have the funds to rent a theater, you can use Tugg, an online resource, to crowdsource theater space. The way it works is you have to sell a certain amount of tickets to a screening, and if you do, your chosen theater will show your movie. You won't make money out of it, but you will have the chance to have your movie shown in a theater without paying for it.

It's even possible, if you are willing to do the work, to plan screenings in different cities in order to create buzz for your film. In this way, you're creating your own festival-like screenings. The difference is you're going to have to do the work of getting an audience to the theaters.

Even if you are so lucky as to secure a slot at a major festival, don't think your work is over. In fact, preparing for a festival premier is rather like organizing your shoot. It's a whole production, and to make the most of the opportunity, you really need to do your work.

The festival will require a lot from you: posters, DVD copies for press, publicity shots, and a press kit. And of course, while they help somewhat with costs of attending, they don't fully cover it. Sundance currently provides a stipend of $2,500, which realistically won't even cover accommodation for the entire festival. Hence it's not uncommon to see crowdfunding campaigns to cover the costs of a festival.

If you've made it into a top fest, you'll be wondering if you need a sales agent and whether to hire a PR person.

First, you only need a sales agent if you are hoping to sell the film. If you plan to self-distribute it, you don't need one, though it's worth having a lawyer at the ready just in case you do receive an enticing offer for it.

The benefits of having a sales agent is that they have pre-existing relationships in the film distribution world, and a good sales agent will have a clear idea of where they think your film will fit. Some sales agents work for large agencies (i.e., UTA), some work for companies that also produce films, and some are more boutique. The deals they offer vary greatly some will ask for money up front (Avoid them! They should only get paid if they make a sale), others will ask for 10–25% of the sale, usually with a minimum built in (anything from $15,000–$50,000). When you add their expenses, be clear this means that you could sell your film and end up with nothing to show for it.

If you get into a major festival, sales agents will reach out to you. If you're not premiering at a major festival, you'll be reaching out to them. In either case, if you do go down the sales agent route, look for someone who is really passionate about your film, and who is going to be extremely proactive about selling it. If they're going to rep a ton of films at your fest, and yours is the least star-driven, be careful about signing with them unless they seem particularly excited about your movie and its prospects.

If you think your film has a good shot at foreign sales, a sales agent will be essential. Look for someone with experience in the foreign markets, and be sure that they have the connections needed to make these deals. Don't have unrealistic expectations; foreign sales deals have plummeted in recent years, so unless you have a meaningful name cast, or a strong genre hook, you can pretty much forget about it.

Hiring a PR representative is important, but can also be challenging. For a Sundance premier, expect to pay $7,000 or more. Have a very clear idea of the purpose of your publicity at the festival. If you're planning to self-distribute the movie, and are launching it soon after the festival, you will want maximum exposure to the movie-going public. On the other hand, if you want to sell it to a distributor, your goal is to heighten its standing within the industry, but probably hold back the excitement for the general public (given that they will have forgotten about your film by the time it comes out). Before you hire anyone, talk to them about their contacts, and what they can specifically bring to the table. The reality is, unless you have stars in your film, the general press will not be very interested in it. Again, you need to find a PR person who really loves your film, gets it, and who will be able to connect it with the right press people.

When my film *Obselidia* got in to Sundance, it seemed like such a miracle that I knew immediately I wanted everyone who had worked on the film to be there. We rented a big house in Park City for the entire cast and crew, and stocked it with a ton of beer and food. The result was nearly everyone who worked on the film came to the festival and had a blast. After each of our screenings, we had the whole gang come up on the stage, and it was wonderful to share that experience. I suspect we were the only film there that had even their gaffer and grip up on stage! Aside from being super fun, if you have a limited publicity budget, having a big gang at the festival helps, as they are inevitably telling everyone they meet about your film. You create your own buzz.

No matter where you premier, make sure you enjoy it. It can be super overwhelming, and you can feel like you've been thrust into a popularity contest that you had no desire to be a part of. The day that *Obselidia* premiered at Sundance, I was racked with nerves. During the screening, my neck was in agony, locked with tension. I was aware of every little noise in the theater, where nearly 800 people sat, and I was conscious of every flaw in my film like never before. Afterwards, we hosted a party in our house, and I proceeded to get drunk quickly and pass out exhausted (happy to say that I did make it back to my own bed!). The next day, I woke up and immediately Googled our film. I wanted to see if there were any reviews. There was. One. And it said (this is tattooed on my battered heart forever): *"Obselidia: A Compendium of Indie Cliches."* I just about died. The review went on to savagely trash my film in the most brutal way.

I was shocked. I thought people might find my film a little dull (not much happens in it, and it is deliberately slow paced), but I didn't expect the meanness of this review (written, of course, by a wannabe-filmmaker/blogger). For an hour or so, I just wanted to leave Sundance and go home. It was too intense. I felt like my heart was being judged; I'd made the film with a totally humble and pure attitude, and I wasn't prepared for this.

My husband convinced me to wait until I after I had attended the director's brunch that day. It's a tradition there that all the directors are invited to a brunch hosted by Robert Redford at the Sundance resort (about an hour away from Park City). No one else is allowed to go; no producers, no agents, no actors. Just the directors.

So I went to the brunch, even though I was still pretty despondent. After arriving, I soon met with the other directors who had feature narratives there, and I found myself chatting with Mark Ruffalo (whose directorial debut was screening). He asked me what my film was, and I told him, muttering, "but you probably want to skip it as apparently it's a compendium of indie clichés."

He looked at me like I was nuts, "You read the reviews?! Are you crazy? You don't read the reviews. You made your movie! You did it! Those assholes don't make movies! You didn't make it for them! Fuck them!"

Two days later, Mark came to see my movie. He's not just an incredibly gifted actor; he's also a solid human being, because he was right. After his lecture, I took his advice (would you ignore the advice of the Hulk?!). I decided to hell with it all, I had a movie at Sundance, and I was going to enjoy it. After that, I didn't read any of the reviews. I just had a blast—screw the press.

However just as the festival was coming to a close, I started getting a ton of text messages:*" Have you seen Variety?! Congrats!!!"* At first, I refused to look at it. If you're not going to take the bad, you can't take the good! But when the tenth person asked me, I caved and read the Variety round up of Sundance by Todd McCarthy. The theme of Sundance that year was "To Rebel," and he singled out my film as the only one that deserved to be called a rebel. He loved the movie, even as he acknowledged its flaws.

I'm telling you all this because I think it's important to have a strategy about dealing with press if you find yourself at a big fest. Bad reviews can be soul destroying, but equally glowing ones can be unhelpful. Be aware of the critics and outlets that you respect. Intelligent reviewers who have a respect for the craft of filmmaking can contribute hugely to your growth as a filmmaker. Reviews by bloggers, who often take pride in being vitriolic and mean, can derail you.

Ultimately though, no matter what anyone says, remind yourself that you made a movie. You got in the ring and risked it all, and no one can take that away from you. If you find yourself getting a lot of press, I recommend printing up this quote by Theodore Roosevelt and pinning it to your wall:

"It is not the critic who counts; not the man who points out how the strong man stumbles, or where the doer of deeds could have done them better. The credit belongs to the man who is actually in the arena . . . who at the best knows in the end the triumph of high achievement, and who at the worst, if he fails, at least fails while daring greatly, so that his place shall never be with those cold and timid souls who neither know victory nor defeat."

Yes, you got in the arena and gave it your best shot, and those critics will never do that.

Once you've made a film, you'll never be mean about anyone's indie film again, because you respect how much work, devotion, and sacrifice it takes. No one sets out to make a bad movie, but it's incredibly hard to make a great one. Cultivating an attitude of support to fellow filmmakers is crucial, as is being kind to yourself.

Remind yourself too, if you've entered your film into a dozen fests, and it has been rejected from all of them, that it doesn't mean your film is bad. If you get the validation of a major one, you'll find that all the smaller ones will pursue you. On the other hand, if your film doesn't get that validation, often the smaller ones are afraid to take the risk with your film. It can be very hard receiving all those rejection emails; I know, because I've had that experience too.

The important thing is that you don't lose heart. Keep applying to fests and widening your net if you want to, but be aware that the approval of festivals isn't necessary for getting an audience to watch your film. You can get it out, with or without them. Be strong, and remind yourself that collecting rejections is a badge of honor for any artist worth their salt. Don't let it get you down.

STEP 15 CHECKLIST

- ☐ Research festivals before shelling out for submission fees.

- ☐ Be ambitious, but don't be gutted if you don't make the cut for a coveted fest.

- ☐ Be tenacious, and wear your rejections as an artist's badge of honor

- ☐ Be grateful for the journey you are on. Go to a festival for your premier, bring all your cast and crew and celebrate. You did it!!!

STEP 16
EXECUTE YOUR DISTRIBUTION PLAN

"Any release is better than none."

CHRISTINE VACHON
auteur producer of *Kids, Velvet Goldmine,* and *Boys Don't Cry*

NOTICE THIS CHAPTER isn't called "Plan Your Distribution". If you start planning now, you're starting too late. Ideally, you started to think about your distribution strategy before you even shot your film.

Now, it's just time to put it into action.

The first thing to say about indie film distribution is that this is a game that is changing all the time, at a crazy pace, so by the time this book is printed, I suspect it will already be different. What I will say is: There has never been a better time to be an indie filmmaker, as not only can you make a film for very little money because of developments in technology, but you can also distribute it yourself in a meaningful way.

The old conventional model for distribution of an indie was this: Your film gets into a festival, and you cross your fingers and hope some distributor will come along and write a big fat check for you, and you never have to worry about your film again. This is literally the equivalent of hoping to win the lottery twice (the first win: getting into a major festival, the second win: selling the film for seven figures). It could happen, and congratulations if it does, but you can't make winning the lottery twice your plan.

Confession: This is exactly what I did with my first film. After it got into Sundance, I thought we'd sell it and be done. I learned the hard way that this was not a good strategy. We did have offers, but none of them made sense. The best one? $25,000 up front, and sign away all rights to our film. What was the point?

Of course, this was 2010, when only 10% of Sundance films got distribution deals. Compare that to 2015 when 80%

did. What changed in that time? Two words: digital streaming. Now Amazon, Netflix, and Hulu have swept in as saviors of the indie film world. It's great, but let's still be clear: that's 80% of the films that got into Sundance in 2015 (2,309 narrative features were submitted but just 77 made the cut). What about the 2,232 films that didn't get into Sundance? What are the hopes for them?

Even with the distribution deals that films do make, it's worth looking at what they're really worth. Naturally, filmmakers want to make their projects look successful, so that they can do it again. But the fact is a lot of so-called "distribution deals" that are announced in the trades are actually service deals, whereby the filmmaker is paying for the release. Or the rights to the film are acquired by the distributor, with very little or no money paid upfront to the filmmaker.

In some cases, this is fine because the company buying the film is Fox Searchlight, and they are going to spend millions in publicity and advertising and mount an Oscar campaign. So sure, you're not going to make any money, but the level of your career will be raised in a serious way. But most of the time, it means that the distributor acquires all rights to your movie, and they will do very little with it—perhaps a one-week theatrical release, followed by it disappearing into obscurity on Netflix.

Not only do you not get any money (because believe me, no matter what it says about your backend, with their expenses and creative accounting, unless your movie does gangbusters at the box office, you are not going to get any money), you are also not going to have the chance for your film to connect with the audiences who would love it, because no one is going to do the work to make that happen. And it is work.

Many times, I have seen filmmakers sign away the rights to their films, only to see the distributors change the title of it and rebrand it. Distributors are often lazy; they want to fit your film into a box they have sold successfully before. So your quirky indie dramedy is suddenly repackaged as a mainstream romantic comedy. The problem with this is that the people who would have loved your movie aren't going to watch it, and the people who watch it will probably hate it. Clearly, a situation that is not helpful for you as you build your career and brand as a filmmaker.

What I strongly recommend is that instead of hoping for a big sale and then taking *any* sale so that you can get your film out there, you plan your own distribution. You work with a DIY distribution consultant, hire a PR person and a theater booker, and start planning how you are going to release your film yourself. You plan so that the day after your festival premier, your film is available to stream online via Vimeo or Amazon Direct.

This doesn't mean you can't change your plan. If your film triggers real excitement amongst distributors, and you're suddenly experiencing a bidding war for it, awesome! Take the best deal and celebrate. But if your film doesn't excite them, you have you're A-plan in place, and you're ready to connect your movie with its audience and make money from it.

Currently, Vimeo allows you to sell your film for whatever price you want, and ... you keep 90% of the price. It's a total revolution. You could be selling rentals of your film for the same price as a festival ticket ($15) and keeping 90% of each one sold ($13.50 per viewing).

Be aware that to really capitalize on the possibilities of online streaming, you want to be able to offer deluxe "bundles". These, like DVD extras, might include deleted scenes, your concept trailer, and "Behind the Scenes" footage from the shoot. You might also include previous films you have made, if you own the rights to them.

The key here is you want to monetize your work, so that your investors get paid back and you make some money too. Also, you want to connect it with an audience who will love it, and build your audience . . . so they will support your next film.

Remember that this movie isn't the be all and end all—what you are aiming for is the opportunity to make a career in filmmaking, and have the chance to make another and another. Obviously that next film will be easier if this is one is a success, but you want to create the circumstances so that even if you don't knock it out of the park with this one, it's a positive experience.

You can learn a lot by studying what other filmmakers do, and you'll regularly find articles in the likes of *Indiewire* and *Filmmaker* in which producers share their journey with distribution. Read these as much as possible and learn.

For me, the way that Shane Carruth handled his movie *Upstream Color* was genius and totally inspiring. The film premiered at Sundance, and he used that as its distribution premier. He didn't go there looking for a buyer, but instead leveraged the attention he got at the festival into audience excitement. He had already made a plan, and working with a theater booker, launched his movie in cinemas shortly thereafter. It went on to gross nearly $500,000. Who knows how much it made through streaming and VOD?

Part of the key to his success: He made a very specific, niche film. He didn't try to compete with the mainstream. He offered something that is not being offered often and sold it as this. He didn't try to water it down in the publicity and make it seem less risky. Serving up cheap versions of studio fare is not a ticket to standout success. The studios do what they do so well; you can't compete. Embracing your own quirky heart and making work that takes creative risks will give you a better chance of success.

After the success of *Upstream Color*, Carruth said, "I'll never have to ask permission again to make a movie." That is the ultimate goal, and it's possible for all of us.

DIY Distribution

DIY is a misnomer. You're not going to do it *all* yourself (well, you could but it's probably not the smartest idea).

First, consider a consultation with a distribution expert to make a plan for your film. Every movie is unique, and you need to be savvy to what will work for what you've got. Who is the audience for it? How will you reach them? Where do they watch movies?

Then, depending on how you want to proceed, you might also hire a publicity person and a theater booker. Some filmmakers do go ahead on their own here, but be aware that if you do, it will pretty much be your full time job for the next year.

You will plan the stages of release, which might include (though not necessarily in this order):

- Festivals
- Vimeo-on-demand/streaming from website
- Theaters
- Amazon, iTunes, Hulu Plus
- VOD
- DVD/Blu-ray
- Licensed streaming i.e., Netflix
- School/Special interest tours

Prepare yourself for the list of deliverables that will be requested for each of these outlets. It can be expensive to prepare your film to release, so if you didn't properly budget at the beginning for this stage, make a budget now. You know what to do: Raise the finance you need. Run another crowdfunding campaign; go back to investors. Show them the plan of how this final piece of finance is vital to get your film out into the world.

Make no mistake: Self-distribution requires a lot of dedication and work; but if you invest the time, you will see the results. The important thing is that you make your plan *before* you go to your first festival. One of the biggest mistakes that filmmakers make is they wait until they've premiered their film, realized they're not going to get conventional distribution and then scramble to do it themselves. The sad thing about that is their film will never have more attention and press than the moment it premieres. Make sure you harness that in a positive way to sell your film to consumers. That way you have a real chance of making your money back and connecting your film with the people who will love it.

STEP 16 CHECKLIST

- ☐ Gather the team you need to make it happen, and hone your plan.
- ☐ Assemble the deliverables you need.
- ☐ Launch your movie to the paying public.
- ☐ Be grateful for the journey you are on, and enjoy the ride.

VIVE LA REVOLUTION!

"If your dream is only
about you, it's too small."

AVA DUVERNAY
inspirational director of *Selma, Queen
Sugar,* and *A Wrinkle in Time*

I HONESTLY BELIEVE there has never been a better time to be a filmmaker. When else in history has it been possible to make a technically impeccable movie with little money, to connect it with an audience before you even make it, and then to sell it directly to them? It's amazing!

But in order to make it work, you have to shift your mindset. You have to leave behind the conventional, competitive, cynical approach to filmmaking and instead embrace an approach that is simultaneously punk rock, D.I.Y., rebellious and bursting with pure heart.

With true independence comes deep responsibility. Throughout every step, you might have noticed that certain themes come up over and over. The importance of community. Doing things with an open heart. Being grateful and authentic. Working hard and being tenacious. Taking all the big risks and never being attached to the results.

These are the true keys to success if you want a sustainable career as a filmmaker in the modern world. The old model of the genius filmmaker working away on his own, supported by wealthy producers? It just doesn't make sense anymore and was never accessible to most, anyway.

If you want to have a career as a filmmaker today, on your own terms, you have to engage an audience, and enter into dialogue with them.

You have to support other filmmakers, by contributing to their campaigns, spreading the word about their work, and sharing your knowledge and experience with them.

You have to educate your friends about Fair Trade cinema (watch things on Vimeo or Seed&Spark where the independent filmmaker will make real money).

The rebels at one of my workshops: sharing knowledge, empowering each other, having fun, and getting movies made.

None of us can do it alone. You can't be a successful film-maker without an audience, but instead of viewing that in a competitive way, be open to the idea that the more we help each other, the greater chance we all have to succeed. If we share with each other how much money we really made from a movie, if we share the truths of our ups and downs in the business, we empower each other to make better choices from day one. And when one of us wins, we all win.

Adopting an attitude of gratitude wherever you are on this journey is essential. It's easy to get caught into a fear-based mindset when it comes to filmmaking because, with a movie, it feels like so much is at stake. If you make a great one, you win; if you fall short of the mark, you lose. That's small pic-ture thinking. If fear informs your choices, your work will suffer. Plug into the big picture, because here's the thing: you never control the outcome of your work. You only control the intention behind it. The sooner you embrace that, the better your work, and your experience making it, will be.

This doesn't mean that you shouldn't dream of where you want your film (and your career) to go. Of course, you should dream! Make your vision boards, set goals, and dream away. Always be clear what your highest and best outcome would be for a film, but understand that it won't always happen, even with your best efforts, and that's okay. Keep faith, learn lessons, and move on.

It might be worth considering what success really means as a filmmaker. Is it to win an Oscar? Or make a ton of money? Perhaps, and I'm not counting those out, but perhaps it's also to make a movie that really moves people. To make films that connect with people in a profound way, entertaining them, scaring them, making them laugh, think, love, cry, live a little deeper. To make films that create connection in our fractured world.

With this new model, the gates are open. Literally anyone, anywhere can have a successful career making movies. You don't have to move to LA or New York. You don't have to look a particular way or to know certain people. Wherever you are, whoever you are, **you can do it**.

Diverse voices that have been silenced by the restrictive paradigms of Hollywood power can finally be heard. We don't need their permission to tell our stories and make our movies. We can make what we want, when we want, and share our vision and truths with the world.

And that is truly radical.

If we support each other, share our knowledge and resources, we can create an alternative film eco-system, one that reflects our values; not the values of the outmoded system of Hollywood. Movies don't just reflect our reality; they help create it. By making our honest, heart-driven films we can change the world—and that is a dream worth fighting for.

By reading this book, I hope you have been inspired to go for it, and given the necessary tools you need to make it happen. There is absolutely nothing to stop you from making the films you want, to have an awesome time doing it, and to make a great living from it. No more excuses. If that is the life and career you want, go for it! Let go of your fear, start working hard, do one thing every day to move towards your goal, and make your dream your reality.

It's not always an easy path, but when you're connected to others, it becomes a lot more fun. You will find a likeminded community of filmmakers on my Facebook page, Rebel Heart Film. Please share your filmmaking news there, as well as any questions you have. Reach out for support if you need it, to me and to other filmmakers. Together, we can do anything.

Stay in touch, and make awesome films!

STEP 17 CHECKLIST

- ☐ Make movies you love.
- ☐ Help other filmmakers do the same.
- ☐ Be grateful for the journey you are on. Even if it's not how you want it to be, or isn't what you imagined, be grateful. You are a filmmaker, and that is the most awesome thing in the world.
- ☐ Vive la revolution!

RESOURCES

Here's a list of books that I've found especially helpful over the years. This list is in no way comprehensive, but will provide you with good places to start!

Screenwriting
Syd Field, *Screenwriting*
Christopher Riley, *The Hollywood Standard*
Blake Snyder, *Save the Cat*
Christopher Vogler, *The Writer's Journey*

Most importantly, if you're going to write scripts, you need to *read* scripts! Check out this list from the Writer's Guild of America of the 101 best scripts ever. It's a good place to start:
http://www.wga.org writers-room/101-best-lists/
101-greatest-screenplays/list

Positive Thinking For Filmmakers
When you're starting your journey (and even when you're miles into it), fill yourself with positive encouragement, not just film books! Here are a few classics to get you inspired:

Julia Cameron, *The Artist's Way*
Shakti Gawain, *Creative Visualization*
Elizabeth Gilbert, *Big Magic: Creative Living Beyond Fear*
Amanda Palmer, *The Art of Asking: How I Learned to Stop Worrying and Let People Help*
Steven Pressfield, *The War of Art*

Directing

Steven D. Katz, *Film Directing: Shot by Shot*

Christopher Kenworthy, *Mastershots Vol 1*

Sidney Lumet, *Making Movies*

Judith Weston, *Directing Actors; The Film Director's Intuition*

Financing, Producing and Distribution

Gunnar Erickson, Mark Halloran, Harris Tulchin, *The Independent Film Producer's Survival Guide: A Business and Legal Sourcebook*

Stacy Parks, *The Insider's Guide to Independent Film Distribution*

Jon Reiss, *Think Outside the Box Office*

Maureen Ryan, *Producer to Producer: A Step-by-Step Guide to Low Budget Independent Film Producing*

Morrie Warshowski, *Shaking the Money Tree (3rd edition): The Art of Getting Grants and Donations for Film and Video*

Online Resources

There are so many great websites for filmmakers now, with *all* the knowledge you need! Here are a few trusted sources that I turn to:

www.filmcourage.com

www.filmmaker.com

www.indiefilmhustle.com

www.indiewire.com

www.moviemaker.com

www.nofilmschool.com

DIANE BELL is an award-winning screenwriter and director whose movies have premiered at the Sundance and Tribeca film festivals, and are widely distributed. An Independent Sprit Award nominee, she was the recipient of the Alfred P. Sloan Sundance Screenwriting Fellowship and a participant in the inaugural Sundance/Women In Film mentorship program. Passionate about empowering diverse storytellers, she teaches workshops online and in person on how to make a standout indie film and works one-on-one with filmmakers to help them achieve their goals. Born in Scotland, Diane grew up in Japan, Australia, and Germany, and currently resides in Denver, Colorado. Please visit www.dianebell.com for her latest news and upcoming workshops or to contact her directly.

THE MYTH OF MWP

In a dark time, a light bringer came along, leading the curious and the frustrated to clarity and empowerment. It took the well-guarded secrets out of the hands of the few and made them available to all. It spread a spirit of openness and creative freedom, and built a storehouse of knowledge dedicated to the betterment of the arts.

The essence of the Michael Wiese Productions (MWP) is empowering people who have the burning desire to express themselves creatively. We help them realize their dreams by putting the tools in their hands. We demystify the sometimes secretive worlds of screenwriting, directing, acting, producing, film financing, and other media crafts.

By doing so, we hope to bring forth a realization of 'conscious media' which we define as being positively charged, emphasizing hope and affirming positive values like trust, cooperation, self-empowerment, freedom, and love. Grounded in the deep roots of myth, it aims to be healing both for those who make the art and those who encounter it. It hopes to be transformative for people, opening doors to new possibilities and pulling back veils to reveal hidden worlds.

MWP has built a storehouse of knowledge unequaled in the world, for no other publisher has so many titles on the media arts. Please visit www.mwp.com where you will find many free resources and a 25% discount on our books. Sign up and become part of the wider creative community!

Onward and upward,

Michael Wiese
Publisher/Filmmaker